TWEETING DANTE

TWEETING DANTE

One Hundred Days of Tweets
from Dante's *Divine Comedy*

DONALD CARLSON

RESOURCE *Publications* · Eugene, Oregon

TWEETING DANTE
One Hundred Days of Tweets from Dante's *Divine Comedy*

Resource Publications
An Imprint of Wipf and Stock Publishers
199 W. 8th Ave., Suite 3
Eugene, OR 97401

www.wipfandstock.com

PAPERBACK ISBN: 978-1-6667-3810-0
HARDCOVER ISBN: 978-1-6667-9839-5
EBOOK ISBN: 978-1-6667-9840-1

03/21/22

Dedicated to my family, friends, students, and teachers, especially to the memory of John Alvis and Raymond D. DiLorenzo, who opened to me the beauties of Dante. To Dennis P. Slattery, for showing me the way. To Anna, whose love never fails.

Contents

Contents

Introduction

People who know me think of me as a Shakespeare man. In doing so, they underestimate my regard for Dante, which is as great as it is for Shakespeare. I've been teaching Dante's *Commedia* to my students for more than twenty years. Mostly, with the high school students I teach, we only read *The Inferno*[1]; however, I have taught all three canticles to college students and every few years re-read the entire *Comedy*, even if I'm only assigning the first canticle to my classes.

In the summer of 2020, I read Guy P. Raffa's excellent *Dante's Bones*, basically the graveyard history of what has happened to Dante's mortal remains since he died in Ravenna in September 1321 up to the present. I learned a great deal from Raffa's book and enjoyed it so much that I read it again at the beginning of summer 2021. That re-reading drove home the realization that 2021 would mark the 700th anniversary of Dante's death, a year that, in spite of a pandemic that still raged, would see numerous events throughout the world, but especially in Italy, commemorating Dante's passing into eternal life. Some of these events took place on the World Wide Web. I began to think about how I could make my own modest contribution to those commemorations of the divine poet's life, work, and death.

Twitter is a social media platform in which I've dabbled for a couple of years. I don't aspire to accrue a mass of followers or to achieve influencer status. Nonetheless, it occurred to me that

---

1. From time-to-time, my students do ask why we only read *The Inferno*. My answer to them is usually that the first canticle is the most accessible of the three to younger readers. In addition, I do think also that it is the canticle that is easiest for most contemporary readers to get. Although distinctive, Dante's portrayal of the ills of the world remain fairly uncontroversial, with some exceptions, to audiences of our time. However, the visions of both *Purgatorio* and *Paradiso* are grounded in an understanding of the *summum bonum* that many in our time would find suspect, either because they would question whether Dante's portrayal of the *bonum* squares with their own conception of a *summum* or indeed whether any *bonum* could be described as *summum*.

Twitter might be the perfect platform for my Dante tribute. Its limitations of tweets to 140 characters or fewer presented both a challenge and an opportunity to capture the essence of Dante's artistic vision and present it in a sort of shorthand that may itself be poetic. As Ezra Pound, himself a great Dante enthusiast, reminds us in *The ABC of Reading*, "*Dichtung=Condensare*."[2]

Then it hit me: My contribution to the Dante celebrations and commemorations of the 700th anniversary of his death would take the form of 100 days of Dante. Each day for 100 days, I would tweet a selection from his *Commedia*. What that translates into, as those who know would have already realized, would be an excerpt from one of the 100 cantos that make up his epic each day. I would try to make each excerpt, at least from my perspective, a representative moment of the journey he depicts as it unfolds in each canto. In this way, I could not only pay tribute to Dante, but also relive his journey with him in this landmark year. My choices may not seem obvious to others, but they are passages that have resonated with me across the years as I have visited and revisited the poem. They would also have to conform to the length limitations imposed by Twitter and, I hoped, largely reflect the terza rima stanzas of Dante's original composition. I began on 21 June 2021, the date of the Summer Solstice, to tweet the first of the 100 consecutive tweets. If I have missed a day along the way, I may have posted twice on at least one occasion to keep up the proper pace. And, in fact, I did omit a day 19 tweet from Canto 19 of *Inferno*, which I have included here for the sake of completeness. I tweeted out my final entry on 3 October 2021, just a couple of weeks after the exact date of Dante's death.[3]

This idea is not exactly original and was inspired/suggested by similar undertakings of which I am aware. None, however, have used Twitter as the specific platform for their observations of the event.

---

2. Pound recounts finding in a German-to-Italian dictionary the German word *dichtung*, "poetry," translated with the Italian word *condensare*, the implications to him I hope now being obvious.

3. Of course, with the adoption of the Gregorian reform of the calendar some 300 years after Dante's passing, the precise day on which Dante died would correspond more closely to the end of September/beginning of October.

To help my tweets reach a Twitter audience, I started by using the hashtag #Dante700, changing after a few days to #dante700, because it appeared that the second was a hashtag already in use and might more readily win an audience. I then switched back and forth, not really knowing if the two hashtags were substantially different or the same. My lack of experience with hashtags is on display here, since my tweets were largely ignored. Perhaps I should have tried a different hashtag, but what I have done, I have done.

The question of a translation to use naturally entered my deliberations. I decided on the Allen Mandelbaum translation for the very practical reason that I own a copy and also because some of my friends and mentors, such as Dennis Patrick Slattery,[4] regard the Mandelbaum text highly. It doesn't hurt that about thirty days into the process, I found a convenient online version of the Mandelbaum text at the Digital Dante website, supported by Columbia University.[5] The digital version of the text enabled me to transfer the chosen passage smoothly to my Twitter feed, as opposed to having to hold my book open to the designated page while trying to type. In the later stages of compiling this collection, the Digital Dante website became unavailable, and I had to resort to The World of Dante website, supported by the University of Virginia, which also features the Mandelbaum translation.

None of my tweets went viral, although a couple did garner "likes" and one "retweet" along the way. Again, the purpose wasn't to draw attention to myself, but to re-echo Dante's immortal verses, even if in translation, in a way that would reach the ears and eyes of people through a slightly different medium, thereby reminding them and myself of the wonder of Dante's enduring poetic vision.

---

4. Author of *Day-to-Day Dante*. I also have Dennis to thank for the two excellent books that use a similar approach, one on Homer's *Odyssey* (*From War to Wonder*) and the other on *Moby Dick* (*Our Daily Breach*), each of which are made up of excerpted passages with Slattery's commentary, one for each day of the year.

5. This site also provided access to the Barolini commentaries on each canto, a resource that proved extremely valuable to me, especially as I navigated my way through the cantos of *Purgatorio* and *Paradiso*.

INFERNO

Day 1 of 100 days of Dante on the 700th anniversary of his death

When I had journeyed half of our life's way,
I found myself within a shadowed forest,
for I had lost the path that does not stray.

(INFERNO 1.1–3)

*W*here else to begin this journey with Dante than in the middle
of things? When I teach this canto to my students, I always
highlight that Dante describes his journey as one we all share. It usu-
ally doesn't take much prompting from me for them to recognize that
Dante depicts himself here as undergoing a midlife crisis, setting the
scene, in his usual roundabout way, somewhere near the beginning
of the thirty-fifth year of his life.[1] It taxes my resources as a teacher,
however, to help them recognize that this is a crisis where the stakes
are life and death in the most profound existential sense imaginable.
The sense of imminent danger is heightened after Dante believes he
has found his way out of his predicament: a mountain that he finds at
the end of the path he walks, which will allow him to leave the Dark
Forest; however, three vicious animals—a leopard; a lion; and, most
deadly of all, a she-wolf, drive him back down into the darkness. Here,
Dante encounters the ghost of the poet Virgil, who informs Dante that
he will lead the living poet out of the Wood on a detour that will take
him around the she-wolf, but that will require him to traverse the
three realms of the Christian afterlife: Hell, Purgatory, and Paradise.

1. Based on the verse in Psalm 89 of of the Vulgate (Psalm 90 of the Hebrew
canon) that states that the days of a man's life are "three score years and ten," or
in the Latin, "*dies nostrorum ipsi septauginta anni*" (Psalm 89:10).

Day 2

"What is it then? Why, why do you resist?
Why does your heart host so much cowardice?
Where are your daring and your openness
as long as there are three such blessed women
concerned for you within the court of heaven?"

(INFERNO 2.121–125)

A fter getting off to such a promising start when Virgil shows up to rescue Dante in Canto I, why does he suddenly lose his resolve, especially when he really has no other choice as far as extricating himself from the hopelessness of the Dark Wood is concerned? It seems counterintuitive, especially since Virgil, whom Dante reveres, is his rescuer. The story Virgil tells here to restore Dante's courage is seminal to our understanding of the drama Dante portrays and of Dante's poetic. It reinforces the sense that grace has intervened to save Dante, something that transcends Virgil's powers and abilities. After all, if what Virgil possesses of natural excellence could suffice, he himself could have helped Dante evade the She-Wolf in Canto 1 to ascend the Blessed Mountain in order to escape the Dark Wood. But Virgil's reporting to Dante that "three such blessed women," meaning the Blessed Virgin, St. Lucy, and Beatrice, have played key roles in Dante's rescue, underscores Dante's incarnational, hence sacramental, understanding of the world as he portrays it in his poem. Only in a universe in which the Incarnation has occurred could the mediation of grace by three human persons—four, counting Virgil—have any efficacy. One further thought: St. Lucy's involvement here in Dante's rescue usually recalls Dante's devotion to Lucy as the patron saint of eyesight, since his was notably bad; but we can also understand it as a foreshadowing of how Dante's eyesight will eventually acquire superhuman strength as he ascends into the higher reaches of Paradiso.

Day 3

Behind that banner trailed so long a file
of people—I should never have believed
that death could have unmade so many souls.

(INFERNO 3.55–57)

*D*ante's vision of the Uncommitted in the ante-room of the Inferno *provides one of the most chilling admonitions to those who read and study the poem today. How many of us have doomed ourselves to unremarkable lives by being either too timid or too self-absorbed to embrace the great causes and to commit ourselves to something beyond our own interests? That's an especially potent indictment of the world of our time, dominated by a consumerism that promotes an ethic of "Me first." Perhaps that's why Eliot was able to borrow Dante's image of death having undone so many in the opening section of* The Waste Land *with such potent effect, subtly—or perhaps not so subtly—teasing out the implication of Dante's imagery that these people never really lived.*

Day 4

When I had raised my eyes a little higher,
I saw the master of the men who know,
seated in a philosophic family.
There all look up to him, all do him honor

(INFERNO 4.130–133)

In the Citadel of the Virtuous, which Dante places in Limbo, the first circle of the Inferno, he proclaims the presence and eminence of Aristotle among the philosophers who reside there. This is what the salvation that can be found in philosophy looks like to Dante. It is a surprisingly attractive state. The citadel in which those who are so honored reside is ringed by seven moats and has seven gates. I always joke with my students that this is the gated community of Dante's Inferno, but these gates resonate with the seven liberal arts, which Dante understood to be the foundation of learning. The image that Dante creates here indicates the scope of Divine Justice and mercy. The virtue of these pre- and non-Christian sages and heroes is rewarded to the full extent of its merit. And yet, that merit falls far short of the beatitude afforded through God's grace. What takes the reader especially by surprise here is Dante's inclusion of the great Islamic philosophers Averroes and Avicenna, as well as the great warrior and antagonist of the Crusaders, Saladin, among the company so honored.

Day 5

"When we had read how the desired smile
was kissed by one who was so true a lover
this one, who never shall be parted from me,
while all his body trembled, kissed my mouth.
. . . that day we read no more."

(INFERNO 5.133–138)

In one of the racier passages of Inferno, *Francesca of Rimini reports to Dante about the moment when she and her lover (and brother-in-law) Paolo succumbed to the temptations of the flesh. It is a passage of great tenderness that evokes a knowing wink at Francesca's euphemism. This moment in the circle where the lustful are punished, being whirled about by gale-force winds that depict the uncontrollable nature of their passions, also captures the self-deception of those who succumb to the fleshly desires as Francesca insistently describes the lust that overwhelmed her and Paolo as "love," speaking very much in terms that echoes the love poetry of Dante's time. Dante's fainting after this encounter—the second and final time he does so in* Inferno—*suggests how much Dante senses his own vulnerabilities to these passions, especially since Francesca and Paolo's fall was catalyzed by reading poetry. It is a hunch that receives further verification with Dante's experience on the terrace of the Lustful in Purgatory, a place replete with the shades of repentant love poets.*

Day 6

"The name you citizens gave me was Ciacco;
and for the damning sin of gluttony,
as you can see I languish in the rain."

(INFERNO 6.52–54)

A well known glutton in Florence of Dante's day, Ciacco, whose name means "Hog," is also mentioned in The Decameron of Boccaccio. Gluttony is another sin punished by a meteorological phenomenon. The unceasing precipitation of this circle is like acid rain, in that it is corrosive and sterile. It is as unceasing as the appetite for food and drink of the gluttons and turns the soil of this circle into mud, fit for the wallowing of the pigs who "languish" in it. After Ciacco delivers a portentous speech to Dante, prophesying the troubles Dante would suffer at the hands of his enemies, Ciacco's eyes cross and he falls back into an unconscious state that Virgil says will endure until the last trumpet awakens him.

Day 7

"Now you can just see, my son, how brief's the sport
of all those goods that are in Fortune's care,
for which the tribe of men contend and brawl . . ."

(INFERNO 7.61–63)

*A*fter Dante witnesses the Sisyphean clashes of the prodigal with the misers in the fourth circle, each engaging in a mindless joust of clashing rocks, Virgil comments on the futility of making the goods of Fortune the end all and be all. Those who grasp or spend without measure miss the point that what they exert themselves so single-mindedly to acquire cannot really ever belong to them, because Fortune is the goddess appointed by God to keep material wealth continually changing hands. In eternal damnation, the wealth that these souls constantly sought after for the mere sake of getting or spending becomes the worthless rocks which they must now roll without ceasing, stuck in a perpetual clash of wills with those whose vice seems the opposite but in reality is a mirror image of their own.

Day 8

That done, he threw his arms around my neck
and kissed my face and said: "Indignant soul,
blessed is she who bore you in her womb!"

(INFERNO 8.43–45)

*A*nother *figure from Dante's* Inferno *mentioned by Boccaccio is Filippo Argenti, a legendary Florentine brawler known for his choleric nature. When Dante lashes out at Argenti's shade, submerged in the murky mire of Styx, the fifth circle of Inferno where the sullen and wrathful marinate, Dante earns this praise from Virgil. Surely it is a strange compliment, for it echoes the verse in the Gospel of Luke (11:27–29) where some in a crowd of Jesus' followers cry out to him, "Blessed is the womb that bore you." To the casual reader, Dante's behavior here seems anything but Christlike; however, Virgil's lavish praise is meant to remind us that Argenti's noxious behavior and the conduct of those like him are hateful to God and antithetical to the blessedness that Dante seeks on his journey.*

Day 9

O you possessed of sturdy intellects,
observe the teaching that is hidden here
beneath the veil of verses so obscure.

(INFERNO 9.61–63)

*H*ere we arrive at another of the most curious passages in The Inferno. *The demons and fiends who guard the entrance to the City of Dis, the nether region of hell, deny Dante entrance through its gates. The Furies appear on the wall and threaten to bring out Medusa to turn Dante to stone. Not only does Dante turn away, but Virgil shields Dante with his body, covering Dante's eyes with his hands, to protect Dante from this threat. Of course, we may wonder what a shade, whose body lacks physical substance, can do to keep Dante safe in these circumstances. At this point, Dante warns us not to get too wrapped up in the literal and to glean figuratively what Virgil's offer of protection for Dante means. Dante wants to keep his readers' intellects from being turned to stone by getting too caught up in what may seem to be literal inconsistencies and instead to glean the deeper teaching from his verses.*

Day 10

My eyes were already intent on his;
and up he rose—his forehead and his chest—
as if he had tremendous scorn for Hell.

(INFERNO 10. 34–36)

*O*nce Dante has entered the City of Dis, with the assistance of an
angel who arrives, after a moment of anxiety for Virgil, to dispel
the demonic resistance to Dante's entrance, Virgil and Dante traverse
the sixth circle, which is a landscape studded with tombs. Virgil in-
forms Dante that each tomb holds a number of heretics. They glow
with intense heat, but remain uncovered until the Last Judgment.
From one of these open sepulchers—that which holds the Epicureans
who believed that the soul dies with the body—arises the imposing
figure of Farinata degli Uberti, a Ghibelline from the generation be-
fore Dante in Florence. Farinata casts a majestic figure. A curious
exchange ensues in which it becomes obvious that Dante holds this
figure who would have been his and his family's political enemy in
reverence because his love for Florence prevented his faction, having
prevailed over their enemies at the Battle of Montaperti in 1260, from
razing the city to the ground. His love for his city provides common
ground between himself and Dante, even if some of the old antago-
nisms between their parties remain. Their conversation is interrupted
by the shade of Cavalcante dei Cavalcanti, the father of Dante's friend
and poetic rival Guido, who puts his head above the rim of the tomb
to see if his son has been accorded the same honor as Dante. Dante's
response to the father's query confuses his friend's father, making him
think that Guido has met with his demise. Because of this, Dante
learns from Farinata that the damned can no longer know the pres-
ent, and at the Last Judgment, when their tombs are shut and past
and future are no more, they will forfeit all knowledge.

Day 11

"However, fraud is man's peculiar vice;
God finds it more displeasing—and therefore,
the fraudulent are lower, suffering more."

(INFERNO 11.25–27)

*A*s *Virgil and Dante rest beside the tomb of Pope Anastasius on the inner rim of the Sixth Circle so that Dante can become accustomed to the stench of the lower regions of the Inferno into which he is about to descend, Virgil gives Dante a lecture on the plan of hell. They have passed through the suburbs of the City of Dis, which comprises the lower circles. There is a distinctive pattern developing in circles 2–5 that reflects the Seven Deadly Sins, but Dante pivots when he reaches Dis and begins a new pattern. Virgil enightens Dante that the circles he traveled prior to reaching the city walls penalized sins of weakness. Beginning with heresy, the sins of nether hell take on a wilful nature. The seventh circle addresses sins of violence, which are bestial in nature. The very worst circles, however, are reserved for fraud because that vice represents a perversion of the intellect, the characteristic that is distinctively human. In calling out Pope Anastasius, whom Dante characterizes as a follower of the Photinian heresy, he continues the pattern begun in Canto III of indicting corrupt clergymen whose actions inflict damage on the Church and the faithful.*

Day 12

I saw some that were sunk up to their brows,
and that huge Centaur said: "There are the tyrants
who plunged their hands in blood and plundering."

(INFERNO 12.103–105)

In the first ring of the seventh circle, Dante is shown those who have committed violence against neighbors. Here, steeped to various depths in the boiling water of the river Phlegethon, which runs red, a river of blood, he sees tyrants and murderers. Not only is the river representative of the blood they shed, but in its boiling heat it also suggests the blood wrath that provoked their murderous violence. We recall here too that Dante learns these things from the centaur Nessus, who serves as Dante's guide through the first of the circle's three rings. This centaur, with the dual nature of human and horse, provides the perfect image of the effects of violence on the human person. The reputation of the Centaurs for their wild and unruly nature makes the fit even more perfect. One of the things that sometimes perplexes my students is how Dante, a Christian poet, gets away with using all of these figures from classical mythology in his poem. But Dante sees no problem with finding in the Greek and Roman gods and mythological figures a shadowy prefiguring of Christian truth. To Dante the classical imagination is the bedrock upon which the Christian imagination is founded. That may be why so many figures from Greek and Roman culture are found in the cellar of his building. However, we will find them in its upper storeys as well.

Day 13

"Like other souls, we shall seek out the flesh
that we have left, but none of us shall wear it;
it is not right for any man to have
what he himself has cast aside."

(INFERNO 13.103–106)

*T*hese are the words of the pitiful shade of Pier delle Vigne. His act of self-murder, having been toppled from his high position by the envy of others in the court of Emperor Frederick II, has sent him to the second ring of the seventh circle where the souls of suicides take on the shape of gnarled and barren thorn trees. He "speaks" through the wound Dante has made by snapping a twig from one of his branches at Virgil's urging. Delle Vigne here describes the forfeiture of the human form that all the suicides will suffer when all other souls are reunited with their bodies at the Second Coming. His case is especially sad because Dante portrays him as an honorable man sent to extremes by injustice and misfortune. When we read this canto, I mention to my students that Dante had no notion of the ailments understood by modern medicine and psychology that often cause those who suffer from them to commit suicide. Dante adheres rigidly to the logic of contrapasso by which a sin is punished by visiting the extreme logical consequences of the sinner's choice upon him or her. The suicides have rejected the bodies given to them by Divine Providence; therefore, they have lost the right to claim those bodies as their own. Of course, Dante himself will later cause his readers to question this judgment when he and Virgil emerge on the shores of Purgatory in the next canticle.

Day 14

And he himself, on noticing that I
was querying my guide about him, cried:
"That which I was in life, I am in death."

(INFERNO 14.49–51)

In this canto, Dante and Virgil witness the soul of Capaneus, a titanic figure stretched out on the burning sand of the seventh circle's third ring among the blasphemers who are punished for violence against God. Curiously, Capaneus is not a blasphemer of the Christian God, but of Jove or Jupiter. He nonetheless is punished here and remains unrepentant, as his words indicate. Some commentators have maintained that the flakes of fire that fall on Capaneus and the other souls of this ring are an ironic manifestation of God's love (think of the tongues of flame at Pentecost), which to blasphemers and others of their ilk become instruments of torment because of their violent aversion to that love. I find Capaneus' statement a striking summary of the condition of all the souls who inhabit Dante's Inferno. They are here because they are somehow frozen or stuck in their prevailing disposition of sinfulness that possessed them when they died. Their eternal destiny is the result of the choices made in their lives and the actions resulting from those choices. In other words, their punishments are not inflicted on them; they exist in the condition that they have freely chosen by committing their sins.

Day 15

"You taught me how man makes himself eternal;
and while I live, my gratitude for that
must always be apparent in my words."

(INFERNO 15.85–87)

*H*ere, Dante meets his old teacher Brunetto Latini. And what a meeting it is! Found among those who are condemned for violence against Nature, Ser Brunetto's face has been almost burned beyond recognition by the flakes of fire falling on the souls who must constantly move on the torrid sand without resting for whatever perversions they may have committed in this earthly life. The moment is both harsh and tender. Divine Justice is unrelenting, but neither the harshness of the penalty nor Dante's outing of his old master's vices prevents Dante from expressing his gratitude for schooling him in the art of wielding words in such a way as to find undying fame. Ironically, at the conclusion of this encounter, Brunetto alludes to his own ambitious effort to win such fame, the Tesoro, a work whose title would be completely forgotten were it not recorded here in the place where Dante reveals Brunetto's infamy.

Day 16

Faced with that truth that seems a lie, a man
should always close his lips as long as he can—
to tell it shames him, even though he's blameless;
but here I can't be still . . .

(INFERNO 16.124–127)

*A*t this moment, Dante encounters a sight that he himself can't be-
lieve. Having reached the inner edge of the Seventh Circle, Virgil
takes from Dante the rope belt that he has been wearing—most likely
an accessory that indicates Dante was a secular Franciscan—and
drops it over the precipice below which the Eighth and Ninth Circles
lie. In response a hideous figure "swims" up to them through the dark
air of the abyss. Dante notes here that in spite of the incredible na-
ture of what he reports and his own incredulity he must speak out of
the obligation that he took on himself in Canto 1 "to retell the good
discovered" (8) on his journey. It is interesting that Dante invites us
to contemplate the paradoxical nature of the way in which poets tell
their truths using sometimes the most outrageous sounding fictions
while he is on the threshold of descending into the circles of the In-
ferno where fraud is punished. Poetry and storytelling require the arts
of the trickster, but escape the charge of fraud by employing artfully
constructed lies in the service of truth.

Day 17

"Behold the beast who bears the pointed tail,
who crosses mountains, shatters weapons, walls!
Behold the one whose stench fills all the world!"

(INFERNO 17.1–3)

*T*hese are Virgil's words to announce the arrival of Geryon, the monstrous embodiment of fraud who guards the margins between the Seventh and Eighth Circles. He has the face of an honest man and the body of a creature that is a cross between a snake and a scorpion. To Dante's chagrin, Geryon must carry him and Virgil on his back in a spiraling flight to descend into the next circle. Virgil keeps Dante safe by placing himself on the monster's back between Dante and the monster's forked tail. It is wholly keeping with Dante's sense of irony that Virgil has tricked the monster into ascending to the ridge overlooking Circle Eight by dropping Dante's rope belt, mentioned in connection with the preceding canto, a gesture that resonates with Dante's critique of corruption in the Church and that comments on one of the three animals of Canto 1, when Dante tells us "with it once I thought I should be able/to catch the leopard with the painted hide" (16.107–108). The moment thereby lends itself to the discussions around the interpretation of what those three animals represent, but not explicitly enough to settle the question decisively.

Day 18

There is a place in Hell called Malebolge,
made all of stone the color of crude iron,
as is the wall that makes its way around it.

(INFERNO 18.1–3)

*H*aving reached the bottom of the chasm that contains the Eighth
Circle, Dante is ready to begin his journey across its vast ex-
panse. He gives it the name "Malebolge," "evil ditches" or "evil pockets"
because the Eighth Circle comprises a series of ten concentric ditches
in which the ten species of simple fraud are punished. Each ditch, ex-
cept for the sixth, has stone arches spanning over it to allow passage
to the next one. The arches over the sixth, Dante later learns, were
thrown down by an earthquake that happened many years earlier.
The ten ditches of Malebolge mirror the overall structure of the Infer-
no, which consists of the nine circles, plus the antechamber, implying
that the Eighth Circle is itself a miniature version of Hell. This reflects
the gravity of fraud as a sin. My students often question why Dante
ranks fraud as being worse than violence among the types of sin. Once
we consider how the prevalence of fraud affects the world, they begin
to understand Dante's portrayal of its poisonous nature on the human
community, an observation that is as true now, seven hundred years
after Dante's death, as it was in his own time, perhaps even more so.
Consider how detrimental to peace and well-being the falsehoods and
misinformation maliciously spread recently in our own country and
in other areas of the world have been.

Day 19

and he cried out: "Are you already standing,
already standing there, o Boniface?
The book has lied to me by several years.

(INFERNO 19.52–54)

*I*missed posting on July 12 and 13 and, indeed, was on the verge of *giving up the project at this point. Several things distracted me; and, like Dante in Canto 2 of Inferno, I thought continuing the journey would be pointless. Hence, I neglected to tweet an excerpt from Canto 19. That oversight slipped my mind; and, when I returned to the project, I picked up with Canto 20. In reviewing the tweets that I posted, I discovered my error. It was unfortunate because Canto 19 contains one of my favorite incidents in The Inferno, captured in the tercet above. On several occasions, my students have asked me how Dante's poem can be considered a comedy if it's not funny. My reply is to play on them a good-natured hoax by claiming that this incident constitutes the one joke in the* Divine Comedy. *Here, among the souls suffering for the sin of Simony, Dante encounters the soul of Pope Nicholas III. Since Nicholas is lodged head down in one of the many holes that perforate the floor of the third ditch, he can only hear, and not see, Dante. When Dante addresses Nicholas, the deceased pope responds by mistaking Dante for the soul of Pope Boniface VIII, who has arrived earlier than Nicholas was led to believe he would. The swipe at Boniface is palpable. One of my brighter students objected that it's not a joke, but an instance of Dante "throwing shade," pun unintended, I believe. If not a joke exactly, it is the kind of insult that underlies the roasts staged so that a prominent comedian can be subjected to the sometimes savage ribbing of his or her peers. Indeed, the image of roasting here has a painful relevance, since the souls stuffed in these holes have a flame burning the soles of their feet, an ironic reminder of the descent of the Holy Spirit on the heads of the Apostles in tongues of flame at the first Pentecost. The holes themselves are* reminiscent of the baptismal fonts in Dante's beloved church, San Giovanni in Florence, as Dante makes clear near the beginning of the canto. The unremitting logic of the fit of punishment to crime should be obvious: those who abused the faith through the practice of simony suffer in a way that reminds them and us of their initiation into the faith they perverted in order to enrich themselves.

Day 20

they had their faces twisted toward their haunches
and found it necessary to walk backward,
because they cannot see ahead of them.

(INFERNO 20.15–17)

*A*s Dante descends the Eighth Circle, his language becomes darker
and more earthy, as do the images he creates to communicate his
vision. The Fourth Ditch holds the Soothsayers, their human image
deformed. The twisting of their human forms reflects their twisted
efforts to know the future without divine sanction. The vision of these
pitiable souls softens Dante's progressively hardening attitude towards
the sins and sinners whose punishments he witnesses in the Inferno's
nether reaches, and he weeps upon seeing the human shape so dis-
torted. Virgil scolds him for this show of tenderness toward those who
presumed to find out the Divine Will through perverted, and even
diabolical, means.

Day 21

And then—behind us there—I saw a black
demon as he came racing up the crags.
Ah, he was surely barbarous to see!

(INFERNO 21.29–31)

*D*ante's art reaches a new level of grotesquerie in this and the next
canto, the pair of which John Ciardi describes in his transla-
tion as the "gargoyle cantos," developing the analogy that some have
drawn between Dante's poem and a Gothic cathedral. The humor here
becomes scatalogical as Dante focuses equal attention on the sinners
punished in the fifth ditch for the practice of barratry or political cor-
ruption and the troop of demons who guard them: a company of mi-
nor devils that Dante labels the "Malebranche" or "Evil Claws." Each
demon bears a name that brands him as a bestial presence, names
such as Malacoda ("Evil Tail"), Cagnazzo ("Doggish"), Draghignazzo
("Dragonish"), Ciriatto ("Hoggish"), Graffiacane ("Dog-Scratcher"),
etc. The entire company is black. Lest anyone think otherwise about
their coloring, it is important to remember here that the faction of
Dante's political adversaries called themselves the Blacks. Once re-
membered, it's easy to see that Dante intends a caricature of his po-
litical enemies, a point that I will expound in the commentary on a
subsequent tweet. At the conclusion of this canto, Malacoda musters
the company who will escort Dante and Virgil further on in the fifth
ditch with a most unusual trumpet blast.

Day 22

The Navarrese, in the nick of time, had planted
his feet upon the ground; then in an instant
he jumped and freed himself from their commander.

(INFERNO 22.121–123)

In this canto, the detachment of ten demons escort Dante and Virgil as they circle the fifth ditch. Malacoda has informed them that the stone arches that span the next ditch were destroyed in an earthquake that happened 1267 years ago to the day, an allusion to Jesus' descent into the Inferno after his Crucifixion. Malacoda claims that one arch still remains intact and offers the escort to bring Dante and Virgil safely to the place. Dante wants to decline, but Virgil is confident that no harm will come to them. As they proceed, the demons hook the soul of a barrator, a corrupt public official in the earthly life, who has partially emerged from the pool of boiling pitch in which these sinners are immersed for punishment. While torturing this unfortunate soul, they allow Dante to question him. The barrator, an unnamed sinner from Navarre, promises that if the Malebranche release him, he will lure others from the pitch for Virgil and Dante to question and for the demons to torment. The demons reluctantly agree; and, once freed, the barrator leaps into the pitch and escapes his captors. That the barrator outwits the demons demonstrates both how stupid the demons are and how cunning those who engage in this kind of fraud can be. The demons turn both on the escapee and one another. Two of them grapple while flying over the pitch and fall into it themselves. While the Malebranche are thus distracted, Dante and Virgil slip away to find the supposedly intact bridge over the next chasm.

Day 23

At which the Friar: "In Bologna, I
once heard about the devil's many vices—
they said he was a liar and the father of lies."

(INFERNO 23.142–144)

*A*s Dante and Virgil continue on their way, it occurs both to Dante
and Virgil, almost simultaneously, that the demons will pursue
them to torture them for their part in the barrator's deception of the
demons. As the thought occurs to them, they turn back to see the Mal-
ebranche in hot pursuit, at which Virgil enfolds Dante in an embrace
and slides with him down the side of the sixth ditch, barely escaping
from the demons. In this incident, Dante dramatizes how his political
enemies among the Blacks falsely accused him of the crime of barra-
try. Dante's escape here is tantamount to a proclamation of innocence
of the charge that would ultimately lead to his lifelong exile from
Florence, with the demons cast as stand-ins for his political rivals in
the city of his birth. Once inside the sixth ditch, Dante and Virgil
encounter two of the hypocrites who are punished here. The two that
our heroes encounter inform Virgil that, contrary to what Malacoda
had told Virgil, none of the arches over that ditch remain intact. This
is the second of two occasions in The Inferno during which we are
able to see that Virgil is limited in his abilities as Dante's guide and
finds himself at a loss when confronted with supernatural evil.

Day 24

And—there!—a serpent sprang with force at one
who stood upon our shore, transfixing him
just where the neck and shoulders form a knot.

(INFERNO 24.97–99)

*U*pon *climbing out of the sixth ditch with great difficulty, Dante
and Virgil descend into the seventh ditch, devoted to the thieves.
Here the souls of the thieves are attacked by various types of serpents.
In some dramatic descriptions of morbid metamorphoses that rival
any found in Ovid, Dante describes how the attacks of the serpents
result in the thief's loss of his human form. Sometimes there's even an
exchange of forms between the thief and the serpent who attacks him.
Thus, those who in earthly life steal the goods of others are forcibly de-
prived of their most prized possession, their human nature, to reveal
that they became reptilian by engaging in acts of thievery. It is a sight
that Dante claims he himself wouldn't have believed unless he had
seen it. At the end of this canto, Dante is surprised to see Vanni Fucci,
whose reputation was as a killer, not a thief. The meeting reveals that
Fucci robbed a church in his nativve Pistoia, a crime for which an-
other had been prosecuted. Fucci is mortified by the revelation.*

Day 25

Throughout the shadowed circles of deep Hell,
I saw no soul against God so rebel,
not even he who fell from Theban walls.

(INFERNO 25.13–15)

*T*hese words sum up the thief Vanni Fucci, whose arrogance knows
no bounds. Dante describes how Fucci uses both hands to make
an obscene gesture known as "the fig" toward God. The serpents im-
mediately attack him and restrain his hands. Dante comments, "From
that time on those serpents were my friends" (4). The rest of the canto
is devoted to further variations on the theme of the serpents in this
ditch implementing the punishments earned by the thieves, which
ironically reverse their sin upon themselves.

Day 26

He answered me: "Within that flame, Ulysses
and Diomedes suffer; they, who went
as one to rage, now share one punishment."

(INFERNO 26.55–57)

Since we also read Homer's Odyssey in my classes, the twenty-sixth canto is one that holds special interest for my students and me. Many are surprised to learn that Ulysses is actually Odysseus' name among the Romans. We contrast here Homer's depiction of Odysseus with Dante's, as it comes to him moderated by Virgil's Aeneid. We make sure to notice that Ulysses meets his demise on a journey whose goal is towards the intermediate destination of Dante's journey: the mountain of Purgatory, the contrast being that Ulysses doesn't know which island his ship approaches when a storm blows up to wreck it, whereas Dante is fully aware that he must reach its shores to continue on to the final stage of his journey. So an adventure that for one ends in disaster because of his blindness to the Christian revelation becomes for Dante an occasion of grace and blessing.

Day 27

Then Francis came, as soon as I was dead,
for me; but one of the black cherubim
told him: "Don't bear him off; do not cheat me."

(INFERNO 27.112–114)

*D*ante *also devotes the next canto to the eighth ditch, where fraudulent counselors are punished. This time Dante, and not Virgil, speaks to another soul encased in a tongue of flame. Guido da Montefeltro had been a political counselor, much sought after for his cunning. As he grew older, he became concerned for the state of his soul and so retired and became a Franciscan friar to do penance for his earlier misspent years. Nonetheless, Boniface VIII calls him out of retirement to consult him about a strategy for dealing with a political adversary. At first, Guido is shocked into silence; but Boniface convinces him that it is safe to give the pope what he wants since he can absolve him in advance for the sin he is about to commit. As a result, he gives Boniface the advice he seeks and returns to his monastery. When he dies, the scenario he describes in this stanza takes place. This man, renowned for his cunning, is outfoxed by the wily pontiff and thereby loses his soul. Furthermore, this soul is only too glad to tell his story because he doesn't believe that Dante will return to life on earth to be able to retell it. The obtuseness of Guido da Montefeltro, the soul in question, is yet more evidence that these souls have, in the words of Virgil in Canto 3, "lost the good of intellect" (18).*

Day 28

"Because I severed those so joined, I carry—
alas—my brain dissevered from its source,
which is within my trunk. And thus, in me
one sees the law of counter-penalty."

(INFERNO 28.140–142)

*S*ome may find Canto 28 controversial, even incendiary, because of
Dante's description of the punishment of both Mohammed and his
son-in-law Ali in the ditch where fomenters of discord suffer. I have
had some Muslim students with whom this canto didn't sit well. Its
offensiveness to some, however, can instigate some intense, but pro-
ductive, dialogue about what exactly Dante is portraying about the
discord that can tear communities apart. It can also spotlight the un-
usual way Dante and his contemporaries understood (or rather mis-
understood?) who Mohammed was and the nature of Islam. At any
rate, the harrowing punishments of those who sowed discord reach
their climatic moment with the figure of Bertran de Born, who walks
the circuit of the ninth ditch with his head severed from his body be-
cause he set a son against his father. It is in de Born's mouth (in the
severed head swinging lamplike in his hand) that Dante puts the term
that sums up the exquisitely ironic nature of the punishment suffered
by the damned: contrapasso, translated here as "counter-penalty."
One wonders which of our contemporaries Dante would assign to this
ditch given the hyper-divided state of our own society.

Day 29

And so their nails kept scraping off the scabs,
just as a knife scrapes off the scales of carp
or of another fish with scales more large.

(INFERNO 29.82–84)

*T*he concluding cantos of the Eighth Circle can be somewhat mysti-
fying. In the tenth and final ditch of Malebolge, Dante encounters
the falsifiers, among whom are those who posed as others in life for
their own gain, alchemists, counterfeiters, etc. Each soul suffers the
symptoms and discomforts of some debilitating illness—some physi-
cal, others mental. My students often wonder, not only why fraud is
a more serious sin than violence to Dante, but also why falsification
represents the worst kind of fraud. Then we think through the logic of
their punishments, and the light goes on. When it does, they come to
the realization that the implication of the diseases that afflict these
souls is that they themselves have been a disease upon society.

Day 30

I was intent on listening to them
when this was what my master said: "If you
insist on looking more, I'll quarrel with you!"

(INFERNO 30.130–132)

What happens to Dante here is an implicit warning to his readers. He becomes fixated on the fight that breaks out between Master Adam the counterfeiter and the treacherous Sinon the Greek. Each insults the other and, to the extent possible in their physically debilitated state, strikes his opponent. The resulting fracas is replete with the low spectacle of a talk show's staged confrontation or of the matches of the World Wrestling Federation. Virgil's impatience with Dante at being mesmerized by the Master Adam-Sinon incident and his stern rebuke of Dante are also meant for the reader who would become enthralled by and mired down in the grotesque, but fascinating, episodes and images of Dante's horror show. Dante doesn't intend them to be the sort of gratuitous and titillating displays available to us in numerous forms of low entertainment. He means for us to be fascinated by them, not for the sake of the fascination, but for the sake of learning from them in a way that will help steer us on a better course for ourselves.

Day 31

His face appeared to me as broad and long
as Rome can claim for its St. Peter's pine cone;
his other bones shared in that same proportion . . .

(INFERNO 31.58–60)

*I*actually have a photo of this bronze pine cone hanging on the wall
of my classroom. I snapped it on a visit to Rome my wife and I took
in the winter of 2006. We had just toured the Vatican Museum and
emerged into a courtyard reached, I believe, through the museum's
canteen. Upon seeing it, I knew that it had to be the sculpture that
Dante refers to here. In this canto, Dante and Virgil have just reached
the Well of Giants that separates the Eighth Circle from the Ninth. The
first giant that they approach is Nimrod, whose face Dante describes
thus. Imagined here by Dante as the instigator behind the building
of the Tower of Babel, Nimrod is another of the several characters in
the Inferno that Dante depicts as speaking gibberish. The corruption
of language, Dante shows, is one of the effects of sin on the human
condition and another tangible sign that those who sin so as to be
condemned to the Inferno "have lost the good of the intellect" (3.18).

Day 32

I bring myself to speak, yet speak in fear;
for it is not a task to take in jest,
to show the base of all the universe—
nor for a tongue that cries out, "mama," "papa."

(INFERNO 32.6–9)

*H*ere, Dante pulls aside the curtain for his reader again to share
his own linguistic concerns about rendering the blood-chilling
experiences of the final cantos in the ninth circle into words. The sin-
ners that Dante will encounter in Circle Nine, the Treacherous, are
submerged to varying depths and frozen into the ice of the Inferno's
final river: Cocytus. Just as the ice of that lake figures forth the hard-
ening of hearts that leads to these unnatural crimes against kin, coun-
try, guests and hosts, and benefactors, Dante adopts a concomitant
attitude and style of harshness in which all pity for the souls of these
sinners, who would have been better off to have been born goats in-
stead of humans, as Dante notes at one point, dies in the bitter wind
that causes the water of the river to freeze.

Day 33

"You are to know I was Count Ugolino,
and this one here, Archbishop Ruggieri;
and now I'll tell you why I am his neighbor."

(INFERNO 33.13–15)

*A*fter *Count Ugolino's pitiful tale of the suffering and degradation
that the Archbishop inflicted upon him and his sons, Dante re-
veals to us one of the underlying secrets of his poem. When Dante
encounters the souls of both Fra Alberigo and Branca d'Oria in the
region of Cocytus called "Ptolomea," where betrayers of guests are lo-
cated, he can't believe what he sees. As far as he knows, both men still
walk the earth not having reached the end of their mortal existence.
When Alberigo tells Dante that, upon committing this sin, the perpe-
trator's soul drops immediately to the ice and a demon inhabits and
continues to animate the sinner's body until the time has come for the
Fates to snip his corporeal life's thread, he suggests a view that doesn't
align with orthodox teaching about the opportunity for sinners to re-
pent. In this case, however, theology gives way to poetry and reveals
to us that Dante's poem is not so much about the consequences of sin
in the afterlife as it is about the consequences of sin in the earthly life.
The images of sin and punishment in the Inferno are Dante's artistic
rendering of how the choice to sin affects the person's soul in the here
and now and not just in eternity.*

Day 34

If he was once as handsome as he now
is ugly and, despite that, raised his brows
against his Maker, one can understand
how every sorrow has its source in him!

(INFERNO 34.34–37)

*H*ow does one not choose the concluding line of this canto, "It was
from there/that we emerged, to see—once more—the stars" as
the most iconic? That famous coda to all three canticles, "the stars,"
serves as such a signature move on Dante's part that it almost seems
heresy not to use the verses containing that phrase as the touchstone
passage for Canto 34. To me, however, it is Dante's portrait of Lucifer
that serves as this canto's tour de force. The hideousness of the Em-
peror of the Inferno is diametrically opposed to the culminating vision
of Dante's journey: the unspeakable glory and beauty of the Triune
God. The details of Lucifer's appearance here perfectly reflect the cor-
rosive effects of evil upon the creature and upon creation as a whole.
Supplemented by the paradox that Lucifer's continual efforts to free
himself from his imprisonment in the lake of ice by flapping his wings
only freezes the ice more solidly, the image provides the fullest realiza-
tion of Virgil's description of the lost souls of the Inferno in Canto 3 as
"those who have lost the good of the intellect" (18). That phrase that
resonates so powerfully throughout The Inferno finds its completion
in the futility and obliviousness of one whose efforts to make himself
God turns him instead into the king of Hell, the ultimate realization
of "the law of the counter-penalty" (28.142).

PURGATORIO
Day 35

"Now may it please you to approve his coming;
he goes in search of liberty—so precious,
as he who gives his life for it must know."

(PURGATORIO 1.70–72)

When Virgil and Dante emerge onto the shore of Purgatory, they find they're not alone. In one of several famous cruxes of the story, Cato the Elder, the guardian of Purgatory, challenges them as escapees from the Inferno. Cato's appearance signals that Dante will take us in a new direction in this second canticle, one that emphasizes the dual themes of liberty and Divine Mercy. Cato's presence here incorporates another non-Christian figure into Dante's Christian typology. Not mentioned before in the story, upon the opening of the gates of salvation that comes with Christ's crucifixion and descent into the Inferno, Cato has been elevated from his former place in Limbo, the Inferno's first circle, to be the gatekeeper of death's second kingdom. If that isn't perplexing enough, Virgil reminds us that Cato took his own life rather than surrender to servitude and captivity when Caesar defeated Pompey at Pharsalia. How do we reconcile this news with the fate of the suicides depicted in Canto 13 of Inferno? There is an inherent logic, but perhaps the best answer is the one borrowed from Walt Whitman: If Dante contradicts himself, he contradicts himself. After all, his poem does contain multitudes.

Day 36

"In exitu Israel de Aegypto,"
with what is written after of that psalm,
all of those spirits sang as with one voice.

(PURGATORIO 2.46–48)

*T*he Barolini Commentary for this canto in The Digital Dante
reminds us that Dante introduces another song later in the same
canto, a song whose lyrics come from his canzone that begins "Love
that discourses to me in my mind" as set to music and sung by Dante's
musician friend, Casella, whom Dante meets here as one who has re-
cently died among a boatload of souls who have set sail for Purgatory
from the banks of the Tiber on a vessel piloted by an angel. As Dante
sees the vessel approach the shore of the island-mountain, however, he
hears the souls who make up the blessed cargo of that ship singing the
psalm quoted above. Although Dante's meeting with Casella is a mov-
ing and bittersweet moment in the story, I have chosen to relay the
verse that includes the psalm instead because I find it powerful that
Dante alludes precisely to this psalm in the "Letter to Can Grande"
to illustrate the fourfold method of interpretation that he is claiming
must be used to properly understand The Comedy. He explains in
the letter—if indeed it is authentic, which some question—that the
polysemous nature of his poem is based on the four traditional senses
of biblical exegesis: the literal, the allegorical, the tropological, and the
anagogical and goes on to explicate this line from the psalm according
to each.

Day 37

"Despite the Church's curse, there is no one
so lost that the eternal love cannot
return—as long as hope shows something green."

(PURGATORIO 3.133–135)

Since the tone and tenor of the story have changed, Dante seems to undo some of the extreme assertions that he makes in The Inferno. Specifically, in this canto, he seems to modify the judgment visited upon the Betrayers of Guests in Canto 33, whose recalcitrant souls are consigned to the ice of Cocytus even before their corporeal deaths. The words here are spoken by Manfred, the son of Emperor Frederick II, hence, being a Ghibelline, a member of the party who opposed Dante's Guelphs, a casualty of the Battle of Benevento (1266). His presence here in Purgatory, albeit still at the foot of the mountain where excommunicates and those who are late repentant must wait before they can begin their purification properly speaking on the terraces above, comes as a surprise to Dante. As his father was, Manfred was known to hold heretical and atheistic views. Those who vanquished him did not even bury him in consecrated ground. Dante here portrays him as repenting in the final moments of his mortal life. Such is God's mercy that even excommunication cannot cancel the effectiveness of Manfred's last minute atonement, which has won him his salvation, a bold affirmation given that the generally held view in Dante's time was that there is no salvation outside the Church.

Day 38

We made our upward way through rifted rock;
along each side the edges pressed on us;
the ground beneath required feet and hands.

(PURGATORIO 4.31–33)

*D*ante *here emphasizes how steep the ascent toward true freedom is. Of course, there are grace and mercy to help the aspirant along; but persistence is still needed for those who would be free of the slavery of sin, along with its skewing of their appetites and of their loves, deflecting them from their proper ends. The extreme effort described by Dante here still accounts for only a small amount of progress, as it takes him and Virgil only a little higher to a point on the lower ledges of the mountain where they are to meet other souls who, because of their delay in turning away from inferior goods, must still wait the prescribed amount of time until they can enter Purgatory proper and begin in earnest the disciplines of purification that will ultimately lead them to Paradise. Even though the souls in this Ante-Purgatory, as some have called it, still dwell in their imperfections, the predominant tone is one of hope as well as expectation because they will one day share in the glories of the eternal Kingdom.*

Day 39

"I was from Montefeltro, I'm Buonconte;
Giovanna and the rest—they all neglect me;
therefore, among these shades, I go in sadness."

(PURGATORIO 5.88–90)

*B*uonconte da Montefeltro is the son of Guido da Montefeltro,
whom we met in Canto 27 of The Inferno. Buonconte's story of
his death in the Battle of Campaldino (1289), in which Dante fought
on the opposing side, and his repentance in his final moments directly
contrasts with the story of his father's demise, seized at the moment of
death from the hands of Francis of Assisi by a black angel who comes
to claim him because Boniface VIII had misled Guido into thinking
that the pope could absolve him of a sin that he had yet to commit.
The account of Buonconte's death is poignant. He stumbles, mortally
wounded, from the battlefield and dies in a place where his body is
never found, while "uttering the name of Mary" (101). This act is
enough to save him from imminent damnation. His comment about
being neglected by his kin—"Giovanna and the rest"—who possibly
fail to pray for his soul because they believe such prayers will be futile,
suggests that his survivors are not hopeful about his eternal fate. The
story becomes even more poignant when we are reminded that his fa-
ther was robbed of the generous gift of God's mercy by the very person
who was supposed to act as Christ's vicar on earth.

Day 40

We came to him. O Lombard soul, what pride
and what disdain were in your stance! Your eyes
moved with such dignity, such gravity!

(PURGATORIO 6.61–63)

*H*ave you ever traveled to a foreign place, somewhere far from
your home, only to meet someone there who hails from your
city, your neighborhood, your school, your church? Such meetings
have happened to my wife and me in our travels in the most unlikely
places. When they do happen, you experience an immediate connec-
tion, a bond, even if the person that you have run into was a total
stranger before. In this canto, Dante describes just such a meeting
between his guide Virgil and the poet Sordello, who was also from
Mantua. Sordello's is not exactly a household name, yet he was an
important and influential medieval poet, one of the troubadours, in
fact. In the nineteenth and twentieth centuries, the poets Browning
and Pound drew attention to him, but most would require the notes
provided by almost all editions of Dante to learn who he is. Here
Dante portrays him as a noble figure—imposing and dignified. Nev-
ertheless, when he learns that Virgil, whose identity he will not learn
until the next canto, is a fellow Mantuan, his response is spontaneous
and emotional: He rises and embraces his countryman. In this liminal
space, a place of exile still, in which he sits apart from the gathering
of souls who accosted and delayed Dante earlier, the memory of his
homeland stirs in him affection and a sense of connection. One imag-
ines that this moment offers a certain comfort to Virgil, as well. For
him, it must be one of those moments of divine dispensation that he is
granted for undertaking the mission of leading Dante to the top of the
mountain, from which he will be summarily dismissed and returned
to Limbo upon Beatrice's arrival on the scene.

Day 41

He said: "O glory of the Latins, you
through whom our tongue revealed its power, you,
eternal honor of my native city,
what merit or what grace shows you to me?"

(PURGATORIO 7.16–19)

*O*nce Sordello learns that his fellow Mantuan is Virgil, he is ap-
propriately awed. The question that he poses to Virgil is cause
for wonder and one to which Dante seems to want to leave the answer
ambiguous. As mentioned in my comment on the previous canto, this
meeting with Sordello is a kind of reward for Virgil, a moment in
which he can enjoy the honor that is due to him for his outstanding
poetic achievement but not in such a way as to provoke undue pride.
Virgil has just described himself as being "deprived of Heaven/for no
fault other than my lack of faith" (7–8), which seems to rule out grace
as the reason for this meeting as far as he is concerned. Yet in this
meeting, Dante demonstrates how grace and merit work in tandem.
Virgil is there as an act of grace because Beatrice came from Paradise
to ask Virgil to lead Dante out of trouble. But she does so because Vir-
gil's merit, earned through the eloquence of his poetry, has made him
the most likely candidate to guide Dante. His arrival at this moment
of the journey is due both to grace and merit. On the other hand, it
is also a moment of grace for Sordello as much as it is for Virgil. This
opportunity to meet Virgil is a gift for Sordello, as his words make
clear. But it is a gift he has merited because he has graced language
with eloquence. For doing so, Dante lionizes Sordello in his treatise on
the possibilities for eloquence in the vernacular, De Vulgari Eloquen-
tia. So the answer to the question of whether this meeting takes place
through merit or grace is ultimately, "Yes."

Day 42

Here, reader, let your eyes look sharp at truth,
for now the veil has grown so very thin—
it is not difficult to pass within.

(Purgatorio 8.19–21)

*A*s the day draws to a close, Sordello now accompanies Dante and
Virgil to a nearby glade, an area that some refer to as "the Valley
of Princes," as they still pass through Ante-Purgatory. Dante again
addresses us directly with an admonition to be attentive to what is
taking place in this canto. He would have us focus explicitly on the
symbolism of the scene so as not to lose the meaning in the story. But
the canto presents us with an odd sort of pageant that takes place.
Just prior to this verse, the souls in the valley sing an ancient Latin
hymn, "Te lucis ante terminum," that was sung during the evening
office to ask for divine protection from the Enemy while asleep. Two
angels dressed in green then arrive—"Both come from Mary's bosom,"
(37), Sordello tells Dante, "to serve as the custodians of the valley/
against the serpent that will soon appear" (38–9). A few verses later,
as Dante talks to one of the souls assigned to this place, the serpent
does appear only to have the angels vanquish it and then to return on
high. The whole episode is intriguing. What temptation could trouble
these souls, whose troubles and temptations should be at an end? It
is for good reason that Dante draws our attention to the meaning of
what he presents here, for it is a difficult knot, one that will take great
effort of thought to untie.

Day 43

I now made out a gate and, there below it,
three steps—their colors different—leading to it,
and a custodian who had not yet spoken.

(PURGATORIO 9.76–78)

When Dante finally arrives at the gate of Purgatory proper, he depicts his arrival there as having happened in a dream: one in which an eagle has carried Dante into the heavens where he can feel the heat of the sphere of fire that separates earth's atmosphere from the celestial spheres scorching him. Upon Dante's awakening, Virgil informs him that while he slept his beloved patron Lucy came and carried Dante's sleeping form to the threshold of the gate. The gate and the angel who guards it feature some of the most striking symbolism of the poem. However, the detail that always piques the interest of my students, when I present them with a summary of what happens at this point in Dante's journey, are the seven "P's" the angel traces with the point of his sword on Dante's head, which will be erased one-by-one as Dante ascends the seven terraces of Purgatory proper, to which this gate, the Gate of St. Peter, grants entry. Each capital "P" is the initial letter in peccata, the Italian word for sin; and each of the terraces that Dante will visit is dedicated to the purgation of one of the Seven Deadly Sins.

Day 44

They were indeed bent down—some less, some more—
according to the weights their backs now bore;
and even he whose aspect showed most patience,
in tears, appeared to say: "I can no more."

(PURGATORIO 10.36–39)

*T*he disciplines of the terraces of Purgatory may resemble punishments. Those on the terrace of pride circle the mountain bearing a boulder on each one's back, causing them to assume a posture that befits humility. The principle may seem identical to the contrapasso of the punishments for the sins of The Inferno; however, there is something far different at work here. Those punishments were all ironic realizations of the sin committed, a sort of reductio ad absurdum, to dramatize the fundamental unsoundness or, in some cases, the insanity in allowing oneself to fall prey to temptation without repenting the sin. The disciplines of Purgatory are meant to act as a corrective to the sin committed that works by realigning the will of the sinner to conform to the good. It is more a therapy than a punishment, reinforced on each terrace by examples created by divine art of the vice for which the souls are receiving treatment and the virtue that opposes it. These incentives to virtue and discouragements of vice are called by some "the goad" and "the curb."

Day 45

"Even as we forgive all who have done
us injury, may You, benevolent,
forgive, and do not judge us by our worth."

(PURGATORIO 11.16–18)

*T*he eleventh canto begins with a bold stroke on Dante's part: a
rewriting of the Lord's Prayer, which the souls being purged of
the sin of Pride recite as they undergo the discipline that eventually
rectifies their wills. The petition in the verse I chose for my tweet on
Day 45 seems to me the most germane to the condition of the souls
who pray it here on the terrace of Pride and indeed on all the terraces
of the mountain, but the final petition of the prayer holds great inter-
est as well. These souls have escaped temptation and the power of the
tempter over them, so they make the final petitions to be freed from
temptation and evil, "not for ourselves-who have no need-/but for the
ones whom we have left behind" (23–4). And so Dante suggests that
not only do the prayers of the living have efficacy for the progress of
the souls in Purgatory towards freedom from whatever baggage keeps
them there on the mountain, but also their prayers can aid those on
earth with the strength they need. This notion extends the Commu-
nion of Saints to include the souls in Purgatory. And here we may be
reminded why poets were considered the original theologians, because
poets such as Homer and Hesiod spoke of the gods. But Dante as a
poet here reminds us that the human community spans numerous
spaces, times, dimensions, and states of existence.

Day 46

He led us to a cleft within the rock,
and then he struck my forehead with his wing;
that done, he promised me safe journeying.

(PURGATORIO 12.97–99)

*A*fter Dante has experienced fully the terrace of Pride, including
*A*ssuming the posture of the penitents as he must stoop forward
*to address one of the prideful who identifies himself as "Omberto,"
and after having witnessed images both of the goad and the curb, im-
ages that are miraculously lifelike, he is ready to ascend to the next
terrace through stairs cut into a narrow passage in the rock. The angel
who greets him at the entrance to the passage touches Dante's fore-
head, as this verse describes. The angel's action erases one of the seven
"P's" that the angel at the gate had inscribed on Dante's brow. These
erasures will be repeated at the entrance to each new terrace. As each
"P" is erased, Dante feels himself becoming lighter, as if relieved of a
burden that he has previously carried.*

Day 47

And my good master said: "The sin of envy
is scourged within this circle; thus, the cords
that form the scourging lash are plied by love."

(Purgatorio 13.37–39)

*A*s Dante and Virgil emerge onto the terrace of Envy, they find
*themselves alone. Virgil takes his bearings from the sun, which is
on their right hand side, and so they turn and move in that direction,
in contrast to the descent into the Inferno during which the pilgrim
and his guide circled almost always to the left.*[2] *As they walk along,
they hear voices that proclaim several phrases taken from both bib-
lical and secular sources that represent exemplary instances of love
shown for others. On this terrace, these voices represent the goad that
is meant to cure the sin of envy by administering salutary doses of the
virtue that opposes the vice.*

2. To digress briefly, my students always wonder what is significant about
the constant circling to the left that defines Dante and Virgil's path through the
Inferno. The rationale lies in the traditional association of the left hand side
with the sinister. However, on one occasion a very insightful student of mine
from several years ago offered another intriguing explanation: He informed
us that the defenders of medieval castles would typically descend the winding
stairs of the castle's towers while fighting off invaders on the left hand side so as
to have their right hands free to use their swords to hold their attackers at bay.

Day 48

"From what I've sown, this is the straw I reap:
o humankind, why do you set your hearts
there where our sharing cannot have a part?"

(PURGATORIO 14.85–87)

These are words that the spirit of Guido del Duca speaks to Dante immediately after denouncing himself as one of the envious whose vice, though repented of, brings them to this terrace of the mountain to suffer its corrective discipline, the sewing shut of the eyes of the penitents. Guido laments the distortion of human desires that would lead people to begrudge others of the goods that can bring them prosperity and joy. Dante seems to touch on here a principle of human behavior that Rene Girard would later expound in his philosophy, based on mimetic desire. Girard posited that our own desires are inflamed when we see the goods another enjoys simply because they are valued by the one who has them. In other words, something hardwired in us makes us desire the very thing we cannot have, setting our "hearts/there where our sharing cannot have a part." As Virgil makes clear when Dante asks for clarification in the next canto, possession of earthly goods entails a zero sum game. The more there is of mine, the less there is of yours. This setting of our hearts on earthly or material goods in turn is what tears communities apart and sets tribe against tribe, city against city, nation against nation.

Day 49

We climbed, already past that point; behind us,
we heard "Beati misericordes" sung
and then "Rejoice, you who have overcome."

(PURGATORIO 15.37–39)

*T*his passage brings Dante's pilgrimage to another transitional
point as he climbs to the next terrace: that which is devoted to
anger. While he is still on the terrace of envy, Dante's eyes are dazzled
first by the sun that is already setting in the direction that he and
Virgil walk, then by the angel who invites them to the opening of the
ascent to the next terrace. Thus, Dante partakes of a purification of
his eyesight, just as the envious souls are having theirs corrected by
sewing their eyelids shut. As on the terrace of Pride the angelic gate-
keeper blots one "P" from Dante's brow with a blow from his wing,
so the angelic guardian here erases a second "P" from Dante's fore-
head in some way that Dante leaves obscure. Does the radiance of
the angel's appearance lift the letter from his brow? And what of the
singing that accompanies Dante and Virgil on their climb to the next
terrace? The quote from the Beatitudes ("Blessed are the merciful, for
they shall obtain mercy." Matthew 5:7) is in the Latin Vulgate, but the
verse that follows in the last line of this verse appears in Italian. The
source of the singing is also unclear: Is it the angel? the penitents on
the terrace of envy? a general acclamation of all in Purgatory as will
happen later with the freeing of Statius from the mountain in Canto
20? Dante may leave these questions unanswered, but it is clear that
Dante's climb grows easier as he progressively lightens the burden of
sin that draws all who live in sin down to the very center of gravity at
the bottom of the Inferno.

Day 50

"Master, are those whom I hear, spirits?" I
asked him. "You have grasped rightly," he replied,
"and as they go they loose the knot of anger."

(PURGATORIO 16.22–24)

*C*anto 16 of Purgatorio *marks the halfway point of Dante's poem.
Once Dante and Virgil emerge on to the third terrace, reserved
for the correction of the wrathful, they are engulfed in a cloud of
smoke that blankets the terrace and blinds them. Although the air is
smoky, Dante's symbolism here is clear. The smoke that pollutes the
atmosphere of the terrace is an external image of the effects of wrath
on the souls of those who are disposed to unrestrained anger. Their
passion clouds their reason and prevents clarity of thought exactly as
the smoke blinds Dante and, presumably, all of the penitent spirits on
this terrace. They "loose the knot of anger" by living in and with the
condition to which they had surrendered themselves in their earthly
lives, being treated homeopathically with a dose of the very malady
that ails them.*

Day 51

"The natural is always without error,
but mental love may choose an evil object
or err through too much or too little vigor."

(Purgatorio 17.94–96)

*Still capitalizing on the strategic importance of the halfway mark
of his story and of the journey, Dante seizes on an opportunity to
set out the organizing principle of his vision of Purgatory, much as
in Canto 11 of Inferno, Virgil lectures Dante on the plan of Hell and
its punishments. As in Inferno, Virgil and Dante have paused their
journey. After climbing to the next terrace, with the erasure of a third
"P" from Dante's forehead by the angel that guards the ascent from the
terrace of Wrath, the setting of the sun deprives Dante of his power to
carry on. While he and Virgil succumb to their imposed rest, Dante
asks Virgil which sin is purged on the terrace they have just reached.
Virgil replies that before he answers that question, he may as well ex-
plain the guiding principle that organizes the terraces of the mountain.
Virgil's discourse identifies love as the source of all action. The tweeted
stanza above develops this truth by analyzing the kinds of love we
experience. Of the two main species of love, only voluntary love, as op-
posed to natural love can go awry. "Mental love" can stray in two basic
ways: Either it chooses the wrong object or chooses the proper object
and pursues it with too much or too little ardor. The twofold division
that becomes tripartite, then, provides the rationale for the organiza-
tion of sins on the mountain's terraces. Love of the wrong object takes
the form of pride, envy, or anger, represented on the lower terraces
of the mountain. Love of the proper object pursued without sufficient
ardor will find its corresponding sin on the terrace where they have
arrived: the terrace of sloth. Love of the proper object pursued with too
much vigor will constitute the sins of avarice, gluttony, and lust.*

Day 52

Following them, the others cried: "Quick, quick,
lest time be lost through insufficient love;
where urge for good is keen, grace finds new green."

(PURGATORIO 18.103–105)

*O*n the terrace of sloth or, better, acedia, a kind of spiritual apathy or ennui, Dante has the briefest encounter with any of the souls he meets in Purgatory. The group approaches Dante and Virgil at a run, putting on the haste that counters the laziness of sloth. They barely even stay to identify themselves or to help Dante find the next point of ascent on the mountain. Dante devotes to his stay on the terrace of sloth less space—not even one full canto—than he does to any other terrace. Thus, he mimics the haste of the souls here who purify themselves of the insufficiency of the love that had prevented them from answering the call to act on and embrace the promptings of charity in their earthly lives.

Day 53

"As avarice annulled in us the love
of any other good, and thus we lost
our chance for righteous works, so justice here
fetters our hands and feet and holds us captive"

(PURGATORIO 19.121–124)

*T*he terrace of avarice or greed is the first on which Dante will
encounter the souls of those who love the proper object but in an
excessive way. Prior to arriving on this terrace, however, Dante sleeps,
since he is prevented from continuing on his journey because the sun
has not yet risen. Here, in his second of three dreams while in Purga-
tory, Dante has a vision of an alluring woman who describes herself
as a siren—the very siren who claims to have diverted Ulysses on his
journey. In the dream, with the intervention of a second woman, one
with a more blessed and heavenly demeanor, Virgil strips away the
alluring garments of the siren to reveal ugliness and filth, with an
awful stench rising from the siren's belly. It is this stench that awakens
Dante, although Virgil tells Dante that he has unsuccessfully been try-
ing to wake him for some time since the sun has already risen, perhaps
a vestige of the effect of sloth on Dante as he lingers on that terrace.
The Siren in the dream has been interpreted as a symbolic figure of
the earthly goods that are the basis of the disordered loves of the final
three terraces. When Dante and Virgil find the cleft in the rock that
will lead them to the next terrace and the angel who guards it removes
yet another "P" from Dante's brow, they arrive to find the souls lying
prostrate, bound to the floor and weeping profusely. The spirit whom
Dante encounters and addresses, that of Pope Adrian V, explains to
Dante the principle of purification that helps these souls sever their
attachment to earthly good, such as wealth and the desire for prestige.

Day 54

Just like the shepherds who first heard that song,
we stood, but did not move, in expectation,
until the trembling stopped, the song was done.

(PURGATORIO 20.139–141)

*A*s Dante and Virgil traverse the fifth terrace in a canto that begins
with a denunciation of the wolf who visits the destructive power
*of greed upon the world—the same wolf that had prevented Dante's
climb up the mountain in Canto 1 of Inferno—they feel the mountain
of Purgatory tremble. Dante has just been talking to Hugh Capet, the
ancestor of the Bourbon kings of France, who has both decried the
corruption of his descendents and informed Dante that the souls on
this terrace themselves voice examples both of generosity and of ava-
rice that serve as the goad and curb of their sin. As Purgatory shakes
the spirits cry out "Gloria in excelsis Deo," the chorus of the angelic
choir that sang for the shepherds at the Nativity. Dante knows that
something momentous has happened, but he will not find out exactly
what until the next canto.*

Day 55

"He who is guide, who leads my eyes on high,
is that same Virgil from whom you derived
the power to sing of men and of the gods."

(PURGATORIO 21.124–126)

*A*s the canto opens, Dante and Virgil encounter a spirit who, like
themselves, walks upright among the shades lying prostrate on
the terrace floor. The soul explains to Virgil and Dante the cause of
the tremor that made the mountain shake a moment before. From the
entrance to the upper storeys of the mountain through St. Peter's Gate
and above, no physical force can disturb the mountain. However, the
newcomer explains, it trembles any time a soul is released from his
or her penance on the mountain and is ready to enter the realm of
the blessed. He himself has been the occasion of the earthquake and
the chorus of the "Gloria in excelsis Deo" that accompanies it, he ex-
plains, and also offers that souls are released when they feel themselves
ready to move on to "a better threshold" (69). The prompt comes from
within their own wills upon feeling themselves sufficiently purified.
The newly released soul belongs to the ancient Roman poet Statius,
who, like Dante, was a huge fan of Virgil's. The scene that ensues here
is one of my favorite scenes in the entire Commedia. When Statius
learns that Dante's guide is the very Virgil he so admires, Statius acts
like a star-struck fanboy. He spontaneously declares his love and ad-
miration for his poetic mentor, and a beautiful fellowship begins that
bonds the three poets, a fellowship that lasts for the duration of the
climb up the mountain.

Day 56

"Through you I was a poet and, through you,
a Christian; but that you may see more plainly,
I'll set my hand to color what I sketch."

(PURGATORIO 22.73-75)

*H*aving *climbed to the next terrace with the removal by another
gatekeeping angel of yet another "P" from Dante's forehead that
lightens him even more, Statius and Virgil become better acquainted.
Virgil informs Statius that his affection for the latter originated while
in Limbo when the newly arrived poet Juvenal informed Virgil of the
great esteem Statius held for him. Virgil then expresses his surprise
that someone so wise as Statius could fall prey to avarice, whereupon
Statius sets the record straight: His failing was not greed, but prodigal-
ity. Upon the fifth terrace the extremes that constitute the opposing
vices are purged, as in the fourth circle of Inferno they are punished.
Again, we sense Aristotle's influence upon Dante's thinking and artist-
ry. Then Statius goes on to recount how a passage from Virgil's* Aeneid
*awakened him to his vice and turned him away from it. Statius goes
on next to describe how the a verse from Virgil's* Fourth Eclogue *that
proclaims the return of the Golden Age, a passage widely understood
in the Middle Ages to be a harbinger of the coming of Christ, turned
Statius toward the new faith that was just being spread around the
world during his lifetime. Dante's portrayal of the efficacy of ancient
pagan poetry in turning the minds of those steeped in it to the direc-
tion of the faith will not strike those like me whose love for old books
and authors helped lead him to the Church as odd. Virgil's twofold
effect on Statius also reinforces the logic both of Beatrice recruiting
Virgil to be Dante's guide and the reason that Virgil can come so far
with Dante, and is even able to enter the Earthly Paradise that awaits
them at the top of Purgatory, the threshold of the Celestial Paradise to
which Dante will continue his journey.*

Day 57

"All of these souls who, grieving, sing because
their appetite was gluttonous, in thirst
and hunger here resanctify themselves."

(Purgatorio 23.64–66)

*D*ante has come among the souls who purge themselves of gluttony on the sixth terrace of the mountain. There a tree bearing deliciously scented fruit with downwardly tapering branches and water splashing on its leaves from the rock above it gives off a delicious odor that causes the souls of the gluttons to feel ravenous hunger that can't be satisfied. The hunger withers them away so that they look to Dante like the victims of an awful famine. As the souls approach Dante, their faces strike him as being so disfigured that he says the features of their faces form the letters "OMO," the Italian word for "man." One of the spirits calls to Dante in wonder at seeing him there. Dante can't recognize the face, but knows the voice of his close friend Forese Donati, who had died only a few years earlier. Dante is astounded that he has reached the sixth terrace so quickly. He says he expected to find Forese on the ledges of the mountain below the gate. Forese attributes his remarkable progress to the fervent prayers and devotions of his widow Nella. He then explains how the therapy of this terrace works to reorder the appetites of those who in their earthly lives were too fond of food and drink. The excessive hunger of these souls is offset and driven out by the deprivation they suffer here. Thus the stimulation of the very appetite they couldn't control while on earth without any likelihood of gaining satisfaction represents a recalibration toward moderation. Finally, Forese tells Dante that there is a second tree that renews the hunger that they feel as the gluttons circle their terrace of the mountain, a tree about which we hear more in the next canto.

Day 58

I answered: "I am one who, when Love breathes
in me, takes note; what he, within, dictates,
I, in that way, without, would speak and shape."

(PURGATORIO 24.52–54)

In this canto, still on the sixth terrace, as he walks along still talk-ing with Forese, Dante meets the spirit of Bonagiunta da Lucca, a poet who recognizes Dante to be a fellow poet. Bonagiunta recognizes Dante as the originator of a new style of poetry the "dolce stil nuovo," whose defining characteristic according to Dante is that it listens for and obeys the promptings of love in the composition of verse. Bonagi-unta was an adherent of a competing school of composition, but there is no discussion of that here. What is remarkable is that Dante turns the terrace on which gluttony is purged to a venue on which matters of high poetic importance are discussed. Why does Dante associate these matters with the cultivation of discipline to rein in appetite? Could it be that Dante's conception of gluttony does not extend to food and drink alone? At any rate, this conversation lays the groundwork for Dante's experiences with the seventh and final ledge, where he will en-counter only the souls of poets among those who walk engulfed within the purgatorial flames that purge the soul of lust.

Day 59

and I saw spirits walking in the flames,
so that I looked at them and at my steps,
sharing the time I had to look at each.

(Purgatorio 25.124–126)

A long the climb to the next terrace, Virgil asks Statius to satisfy
Dante's curiosity about the phantom bodies that the souls of the
dead bear, which seem capable of experiencing physical effects, such
as the thinning to the point of starvation that Dante has just wit-
nessed among the souls of the penitent gluttons. Statius' explanation
begins with an account of the coming into being of the human body
and soul as a baby develops in the womb. It is an account that would
cause anyone acquainted with modern physiology to scoff; but Dante's
method here is not based on empirical science. The explanation is
based on what Dante believed to logical. We may even question how
logical the account is, but that would not be a helpful way to approach
this passage either. Our best bet is to remember that Statius' little ex-
position here is ultimately intended to be not logical, but mythologi-
cal. At any rate, this interlude is the needed preparation for Dante's
arrival on the final terrace, where the vice of lust is disciplined. Since
lust requires the full participation of the body and the enjoyment of its
sensations, some sort of context is needed so that Dante can portray
the chastening of the body for these penitents who walk the circuit
of the seventh terrace through a wall of intense flame that engulfs
them and leaves very little and very precarious passage to those who
would escape the flame dizzyingly near the outer edge of the terrace.
The correction administered here is again a homeopathic one, based
on the natural association between the intense desires of lust and the
sensation of burning to be found in numerous texts and contexts, such
as that of Paul's pithy remark in the First Letter to the Corinthians: "it
is better to marry than to burn" (7:9).

Day 60

Then, to make place, perhaps, for those behind him,
he disappeared into the fire, just as
a fish, through water, plunges toward the bottom.

(PURGATORIO 26.133–135)

*A*s *in other places, the souls here note that Dante's body blocks the sunlight. One of the penitent stops to inquire of his situation; but before he does, another troop of shades moving in the opposite direction arrives, crying out "Sodom and Gomorrah." They briefly embrace their fellows and then move on. Dante here reveals that his treatment of lust will be comprehensive. The one who stopped to speak to Dante explains that the group that moves from left to right, countering those moving the opposite way, do penance over their desire for the same sex, whereas the others purge their lust for the opposite sex. Dante's interlocutor identifies himself as Guido Guinizelli, who wrote verses that were a forerunner of Dante's "new style." Dante reverences yet another poetic mentor before Guinizelli "disappear[s] into the fire." In a remarkable conceit that compares the fire to its opposite, he points out to Dante the figure of Arnaut Daniel, whom he identifies in words famously appropriated by T.S. Eliot to use an an epigraph for* The Waste Land, *as being "il miglior fabbro," "the better master." Then a remarkable moment ensues when Arnaut addresses Dante in his native tongue of Langue d'Oc. Again, Dante's focus is on love poets, who seem to make up the majority of the souls inhabiting the terrace where lust is purged.*

Day 61

No sooner was I in that fire than I'd
have thrown myself in molten glass to find
coolness—because those flames were so intense.

(PURGATORIO 27.49–51)

*T*his canto is a pivotal one in the story because it portrays Dante
undergoing what appears to be the final purification he will ex-
perience on the holy mountain. I chose this verse as representative be-
cause of the vivid and surprising imagery with which Dante describes
the sensation of walking through the wall of flame. The fire cleanses
him of lust and will presumably remove the final "P" traced on his
brow, but first there is a reprise of the moment in Canto 2 of Inferno,
in which Dante almost abandons the mission before it begins. Just
as there Virgil spurs Dante on with the tale of Beatrice's visit to him
in Limbo, so here Virgil gives Dante the encouragement he needs to
submit himself to the fire that he fears by reminding him that Beatrice
awaits him beyond the wall of flame. This exhortation gives Dante the
needed push, and he follows Virgil and Statius into the fire walking
toward the angel who awaits them on the other side. This procession
raises two important considerations, one an observation, the other a
question. Since Statius also walks through the fiery wall, the implica-
tion is that all of the penitents who have been freed from Purgatory
must make the same walk as perhaps the final step of their purifica-
tion. The question has to do with Virgil: What is the effect on him of
experiencing this cleansing flame that will purify the other two poets?
Why does this experience not free him from the exile from God's eter-
nal kingdom to which he has been sentenced? At the end of the canto,
after the three poets are forced to rest in the narrow passage that will
take them to the summit of the mountain and they have emerged on
that summit with the sun of a new day, Virgil absolves Dante of any
further obedience to him, for "your will is free, erect, and whole—to

act/against that will would be to err" (140–1). Why is the same not true of Virgil? With Dante there's never not a reason, but this one is just a bit challenging to tease out.

Day 62

Those ancients who in poetry presented
the golden age, who sang its happy state,
perhaps, in their Parnassus, dreamt this place.

(PURGATORIO 28.139–141)

*S*till in the company of Virgil and Statius, Dante has summited
the mountain and has discovered a place where nature is in its
unspoiled state. Near the end of the previous canto, Virgil tells Dante,
"I've brought you here through intellect and art" (27.130). They have
indeed reached the highest peak that "intellect and art" can achieve.
So Dante speculates that the ancient pre-Christian vision of the Gold-
en Age found in the work of authors such as Ovid could be explained
as an intuition of Eden. In other words, this is the highest point of
the intersection of the classical and the Christian. It is an intuition
that sustains Statius' (hence Dante's) earlier claim that pagan authors
can be a means of salvation, supplemented, naturally, by the grace
that will lead Dante on to more exalted visions and then to the most
exalted of all. And though they may fall short, the ancient dreams of
the pagan authors still hold an incredibly high and esteemed place in
Dante's hierarchy of goods. Dante implies that, understood correctly,
they can be vehicles of a natural grace that can pave the way for the
introduction of supernatural grace.

Day 63

Full of astonishment, I turned to my
good Virgil; but he only answered me
with eyes that were no less amazed than mine.

(PURGATORIO 29.55–57)

*T*he three pilgrims are now following the lead of a beautiful maiden who greets them across a stream that separates them. Matilda, as she is called, is the guardian spirit of the Earthly Paradise. She talks to Dante as they move to the right, against the current of the stream. When they turn with a bend in the stream that leaves them facing east as they look across, Dante begins to perceive a procession led by seven giant, golden candlesticks streaming flames like the colors of the rainbow. Behind them come a group of 24 elders clad in white and crowned with lilies, singing as they walk, followed by the four living creatures of Ezekiel but appearing, according to Dante, as they are described in John's Apocalypse, a Chariot drawn by a griffin and accompanied by three nymphs gracefully dancing at its right wheel and four dancing at its left. Then follow two more elders with grave faces and four after them, with one final elder who appears to be sleeping, all seven crowned with roses and red flowers. Some have compared this pageant to a Eucharistic procession in which Beatrice, riding in a car drawn by the double-natured griffin, which is an emblem of Christ, occupies the place of the host venerated in this rite. As this procession approaches, both Dante and, appropriately, Virgil stand dumbstruck. This vision transcends Virgil's eloquence. He can only stand and see this vision with silent amazement, which is yet another sign that his usefulness as Dante's guide on his journey has reached its limit. A stroke of thunder is heard that brings the procession to a halt, and Dante awaits further developments that will be revealed in the next canto.

Day 64

"Dante, though Virgil's leaving you, do not
yet weep, do not weep yet; you'll need your tears
for what another sword must yet inflict."

(PURGATORIO 30.35–37)

*T*his stanza occurs just after Dante discovers that Virgil is no lon-
ger by his side and that he has, mission accomplished, returned
to Limbo. This moment is a poignant one both for Dante and for us.
We may be saddened that Virgil, who has been so essential to the
story up to this point, exits here, with a little more than one third
of the tale left to tell. We may even be slightly disappointed that, af-
ter reaching such heights, Virgil has not earned a reprieve from his
eternal sentence to the first circle of the Inferno and is doomed to
resume that existence of sighs, in spite of the pleasant circumstances
provided by the citadel that enjoys some measure of illumination and
the company of sages and heroes, some of the "A-listers" of the antique
world. This disappointment may even be exacerbated by those who
announce the arrival of Beatrice with a quotation from Virgil: "Mani-
bus, oh, date lilia plenis" (21). Although Dante weeps, he is unrelent-
ing in his dismissal of Virgil from the story. Of course, one who is
more important to Dante even than Virgil has just arrived to replace
the bard of the Latins. She warns Dante that, contrary to expectation,
his penance has not ended. There is a sin that he still must remit; and,
for Beatrice, it's personal. She is about to dress Dante down for his
infidelity to her when death removed her physical presence from him.
This straying on Dante's part was a grave error because ultimately it
was Providence that put her in his path in the earthly life as a means
of drawing him to the heavenly beatitude, of which her name is a
figure and a reminder.

Day 65

A thousand longings burning more than flames
compelled my eyes to watch the radiant eyes
that, motionless, were still fixed on the griffin.

(PURGATORIO 31.118–120)

*T*he stanza quoted here reestablishes fully the connection between
Beatrice and Dante, which is why I chose it as a key moment in
this canto. Prior to this point, Dante has had to suffer the ordeal of
Beatrice's accusation of faithlessness, the ordeal for which Beatrice has
earlier advised Dante to save his tears. Not only is he forced to admit
that he strayed from Beatrice after her death, but that he also turned
away from her to seek lesser goods, the transient pleasures that the
very fact of her death should have caused him to shun. These admis-
sions take a great toll on Dante, so much so, that after the second one,
he loses consciousness, which hasn't happened since his visit to the
second circle of the Inferno, after the interview with the lovers Paolo
and Francesca. His fainting here after confessing his transgression
again points to his susceptibility to the weakness that damned those
two lovers. Upon recovering, Dante finds himself in the company of
Matilda, who has crossed the stream that divided them. She pulls
Dante into the stream, making sure to push his head below the water
so that he can drink. The stream that she has immersed him in is
Lethe, which gives those who drink from it forgetfulness of any prior
flaws. With this preparation, Beatrice allows Dante to gaze upon her
eyes, the same eyes that had so many years before made him Love's
servant. All this time, her eyes are fixed upon the griffin, whose double
nature makes him a figure of Christ. Dante's gaze thereby takes in the
now unearthly beauty of his beloved's eyes along with an image of the
Creator of that beauty, formed first and finally, for His glory.

Day 66

"Adam," I heard all of them murmuring,
and then they drew around a tree whose every
branch had been stripped of flowers and of leaves.

(PURGATORIO 32.37–39)

*T*he *tweeted stanza for this day marks the beginning of a strange spectacle involving the car or chariot in which Beatrice has ridden. First the entire company changes location. They walk in the Earthly Paradise until they come to the tree mentioned here. Both the murmuring of "Adam" and the barren condition of the tree make clear that it is the tree of the forbidden fruit from which our first parents ate. The griffin ties the chariot to a branch of the tree, at which the tree bursts again into leaf and flower. The company breaks into a hymn whose beauty is so powerful that it causes Dante to swoon. When he comes to again, he finds that Beatrice has dismounted from the chariot, and then a series of events with apocalyptic overtones takes place with the chariot as their centerpiece. As the chariot is subjected to violent attacks from an eagle, a dragon, a prostitute, and her giant paramour, it becomes clear (or should at any rate) that the chariot is a symbol of the Church, which has both profited and suffered from the political machinations of regimes dating back to the Roman Empire. The final insult comes when the prostitute casts lascivious gazes at Dante, at which the Giant beats her, seizes the chariot, and drags both chariot and prostitute away. Some have found in this final attack a reference to the so-called "Babylonian Captivity," during which time (1309–1377) the papacy moved its seat from Rome to Avignon at the behest of the French king, an event that for many in Dante's time must have seemed a sign that the end was at hand.*

Day 67

From that most holy wave I now returned
to Beatrice; remade, as new trees are
renewed when they bring forth new boughs, I was
pure and prepared to climb unto the stars.

(PURGATORIO 33.142–145)

*I*n choosing from this canto, I couldn't resist the iconic closing lines,
*which bring Dante's "second canticle" (140) to a close. The first
and middle parts of the canto, nonetheless, are not without interest.
Among other things, in the initial and medial sections, Beatrice com-
ments on the spectacle of the spoiling and abduction of the chariot
that they have just witnessed. Her oracular statement parallels Virgil's
prophecy of the Greyhound in Canto 1 of Inferno and provides one of
the famous cruxes of the story. It has kept students of the poem locked
in controversy for years. Here, Beatrice foretells the advent of someone
she describes as "a Five/Hundred and Ten and Five" (43–4), who will
come and slay the Prostitute and the Giant. Apparently, this prophecy
portends the coming of a savior, whose name can be summed using
numerology to the number Beatrice names. Identifying the person
whose name fits that number value in a decisive way is a task that
has eluded generations of commentators on the poem. After one final
dig at Dante for having strayed from the way Beatrice would have led
him on, a dig that fails to register with Dante because his dip in Lethe
removed his memory of having committed a fault, Beatrice implores
Matilda to help first Dante, then Statius, immerse themselves in the
second holy stream in the Garden: Eunoe, a drink of which strength-
ens the resolve and the will to align oneself with the highest good.
Dante comments on the ineffable sweetness of drinking from that
stream, stating he would love to describe it but demurs because this
phase of the story is drawing to a close. Only now is Dante prepared to
continue his pilgrimage to its final stages, among the stars.*

PARADISO
Day 68

"You are not on the earth as you believe;
but lightning, flying from its own abode,
is less swift than you are, returning home."

(PARADISO 1.91–93)

From the launch pad of the Earthly Paradise, Dante has achieved lift off to become one of the earliest astronauts in history. As are all of the cantos, this one is packed. As Dante sets forth on the last part of his story, whose exalted destination will tax his memory to recall the salient details, he calls upon Apollo to aid him and his song to achieve the elevated strain that will be needed for the full accomplishment of his task. That invocation and several allusions to Ovid's Metamorphoses *pick up and maintain the theme of the consonance between classical culture and Christian soteriology last seen in the later cantos of* Purgatorio.*The stanza tweeted on this day marks a particularly powerful moment as Beatrice takes on the mantle of being Dante's guide. Dante senses that he has undergone a transformation and compares himself to Glaucus, who was transformed into a sea god upon eating a magical herb, one of the Ovid allusions. What he doesn't realize is that he has been translated into the celestial regions of the universe that surround the earth. Beatrice here makes clear to him that he is now flying into the heavens. She further explains that it would be unnatural at this point were he still bound to earth, having undergone the purifying rituals that have freed him from mundane attachments. She tells him that God has so ordered the universe that everything seeks its natural place in its order. According to her explanation, only their misguided desires for earthly goods keep members of the human race bound to the earth, a concept perfectly in accordance with the way in which Dante couples sin with the downward pull of gravity in the Inferno.*

Day 69

Into itself, the everlasting pearl
received us, just as water will accept
a ray of light and yet remain intact.

(PARADISO 2.34–36)

*D*ante here remarks on his arrival in, and physically merging
with, the first of the heavenly bodies whose spheres he will visit
on his journey: the moon. His arrival is something more than "one
small step for a man," for Dante's account describes an act that would
be impossible on earth, because here two objects cannot occupy the
same space. The sphere of the moon is the first of the nine spheres that
Dante will visit in the material heavens. Everything below the moon
(the "sublunary") is subject to change, whereas everything above it
is unchanging, save for the positions that they occupy as the spheres
move. Accordingly, the souls that Dante encounters in the sphere of
the moon appear to him here because their virtue in their earthly ex-
istence was compromised in some way and did not remain constant.
We will learn more of this in the next canto. In the meantime, Beatrice
schools Dante further on the makeup of the moon and the cause of
the spots, which people observe when seeing the moon from the earth.

Day 70

"And in His will there is our peace: that sea
to which all beings move—the beings He
creates or nature makes—such is His will."

(PARADISO 3.85–87)

*T*o me, this is one of the most comforting moments on Dante's
visit to the celestial realm. In Canto 24 of Purgatorio, Forese
Donati tells Dante that his sister Piccarda "on high Olympus is in
triumph" (15). Dante sees what appears to be a number of reflected
faces within the translucent substance of which the moon is made,
and they appear eager to speak. Piccarda makes one among these
presences that Dante realizes are not reflections but the manifesta-
tion of blessed souls. Those who visit Dante here in the sphere of the
moon are among the lowest ranked of the blessed, however, because in
the earthly life they broke vows that they had taken. Piccarda herself
had been a nun, but her brother Corso (whom Forese predicts will
find himself in the Inferno) removed her from the convent to wed her
to someone who would bring greater prestige and power to himself
and her family. Dante learns that even if one breaks a vow through
force exerted by another, the person who took and broke the vow still
maintains some level of culpability. Dante also asks Piccarda if these
souls do not desire a higher station and a greater level of blessedness
in Paradise, to which Piccarda makes her well-known answer: the
bliss of Paradise doesn't depend on how high a place one holds in
Paradise, but in existing in perfect conformity to God's will. That, in
Dante's summation, explains to him, "how every place/in Heaven is
in Paradise" (88–9). A true comfort to those of us who are sure that
they are not cut from the same cloth as the great saints.

Day 71

"Such signs are suited to your mind, since from
the senses only can it apprehend
what then becomes fit for the intellect."

(PARADISO 4.40–42)

*T*his day's verse makes up part of Beatrice's response to one of the
two doubts bothering Dante after he speaks with Piccarda. This
is Beatrice's answer to the doubt that she believes to be more danger-
ous to Dante, because it may lead Dante to a heretical conclusion.
Dante is still perplexed by meeting the group of souls he encounters in
the sphere of the moon because it seems to validate Plato's teaching in
The Timaeus *that at death souls return to the planet whose influence
governed them in their earthly lives. Beatrice assures Dante that the
souls with whom he has just visited exist, as do all the denizens of
Paradise, in the heaven beyond space and time in which God dwells.
What Dante has witnessed is a sort of theophany in which the souls
show themselves to Dante to indicate their place in the Heavenly hi-
erarchy, in this case among the lowest of the blessed. This has been an
accommodation to Dante's human nature, which relies on sense per-
ception for its knowledge. It's a curious thing for Beatrice to explain all
this to Dante here, since this is precisely what Dante has been doing
in his poem all along: appealing to the intellects of his readers through
the poetic imagery that appeals to our senses. The fact that Beatrice
explains to Dante a concept that is integral to the poetic enterprise
provides a subtle way for Dante to reaffirm one of the essential prop-
erties of his entire work and to bolster it through Beatrice's observa-
tion that Scripture works on exactly the same principle, affirming that
this accommodation has its origin in Divine Providence.*

Day 72

When she had passed into that heaven's light,
I saw my lady filled with so much gladness
that, at her joy, the planet grew more bright.

(PARADISO 5.94–96)

*A*s Beatrice expounds her discourse on the nature of vows and the
measure of culpability the individual bears for breaking them,
*Dante and his guide continue their ascent to the second sphere of
Paradise: the sphere of Mercury. Thousands of avatars of the blessed
meet them here, and Dante will soon enter into discourse with one
who singles himself out from the rest to speak with the visitor. Apart
from the brilliance of Beatrice's explanations, summing up a number
of difficult concepts related to the idea of free will, the brilliance of her
person increases as they move higher into the heavens. Dante here por-
trays a symbiotic relationship between Beatrice and the planet whose
sphere they enter. Indeed, Beatrice grows in beauty and radiance with
each new level of the Paradiso that they enter. This should come as no
surprise: Dante identifies Beatrice with the celestial kingdom through
which they are traveling. You might say that she is the embodiment
of the splendor of each of the spheres they visit. For Dante, Beatrice is
heaven, not in the phony, hyperbolic way of Petrarchan and courtly
pretension, but in the sacramental sense that she makes, and has
made, the eternal glory present to Dante. In Christopher Marlowe's
Dr. Faustus, Mephistopheles makes the statement that wherever he
is is hell. Dante here maintains exactly the opposite with respect to
Beatrice. For Dante, wherever Beatrice is is Paradise.*

Day 73

"This little planet is adorned with spirits
whose acts were righteous, but who acted for
the honor and the fame that they would gain"

(PARADISO 6.112–114)

*O*f the myriad avatars who greet Dante in this, the sphere of
Mercury, the one who actually addresses him is the Emperor
Justinian. It's important to remember that Dante is still in the lower
reaches of the physical heavens, which means that the souls whose
avatars he is encountering are those whose blessedness was somehow
compromised. To account for the blemishes to their blessedness, these
souls appear to Dante through the projections of light arranged by
Providence in the heavenly spheres that are touched by the shadow
of the earth. The souls who appear here devoted their lives, one might
say, to the higher good, but not to the highest good. The Emperor Jus-
tinian, who gives Dante a short course on the vicissitudes of the provi-
dentially sanctioned Roman imperial rule, sums up the pitfall that
all of these souls shared in common—one they eventually overcome,
but not decisively enough to be included among those whose virtue
was truly heroic and devoted to the ultimate good of God's glory. To
paraphrase Piccarda Donati in Canto 3, their souls are not impure.
They were purged of all impurity by any time spent in Purgatory. They
just do not possess the same capacity for the experience of glory and
beatitude that the souls in the higher regions of Paradise do.

Day 74

But Beatrice soon ended that; for she
began to smile at me so brightly that,
even in fire, a man would still feel glad.

(PARADISO 7.16–18)

*N*ote *the recollection here of the final terrace of Purgatory. Virgil encouraged Dante to enter the flame that he feared using the carrot of being able to see Beatrice once he has done so. The ensuing purification and correction of Dante's will so that his previously misdirected love is once again aimed toward its proper end has paid off in moments such as these in which Beatrice becomes ever more amiable and her beauty ever more radiant. Beatrice lights up here because she has intuited Dante's perplexity over what he learns from Justinian in the previous canto about the punishment sent upon the Jews for their role in the Crucifixion, when that Crucifixion was providentially demanded to restore the relationship between God and humankind that was damaged by Adam's sin. The explanation that Beatrice gives seems grounded in a teaching similar to that found in St. Anselm's* Cur Deus Homo, *at least as far as the reason why atonement for Adam's sin specifically required a God-man both to satisfy the penalty for the sin, as a descendant of Adam, and to explain the ineffable generosity of God himself to become that man who would sacrifice himself for us. Dante thereby affirms that the way to Paradise, the "right road" from which he strayed before the commencement of his journey, is reclaimed through paradox.*

Day 75

I did not notice my ascent to it,
yet I was sure I was in Venus when
I saw my lady grow more beautiful.

(PARADISO 8.13–15)

*T*he complementarity of Beatrice and the spheres of Paradise is
featured again in this canto. The aptness of the increase of Bea-
trice's beauty as she and Dante enter the sphere of Venus should be
evident. This planet manifests the amorous feelings that first drew
Dante to Beatrice and reflects Dante's devotion to the subject of love
as a lyric poet. This canto even alludes to one of Dante's lyric poems,
which begins, "'Voi che 'ntendendo il terzo ciel movete'" or "'You who,
through understanding, move the third/heaven'" (37-38), quoted by
Charles Martel—not the Charles Martel who defeated the Moors at
Tours in 742, but the contemporary of Dante who belonged to the
house of Anjou. But to return to Beatrice, the augmentation of her
beauty here, as Dante enters an even more beautiful and luminous
sphere than any he has yet visited, provides another subtle reminder
to us that Dante equates Beatrice with Paradise. Such a move on the
part of the great lyric and epic poet should not surprise us. From the
beginning, Beatrice has been for Dante the personification of heavenly
glory. As Charles becomes the central speaker of most of the canto,
he comments on the members of his house and their various roles in
European politics. Upon Dante's asking about the decline in virtue
we sometimes see from one generation to the next, Charles discourses
on the influence the stars have in molding different types of people
The canto ends with something that sounds as if it could be a gloss
on Shakespeare's Henry VI, lamenting that often we force people
into positions and circumstances that are contrary to their natural
inclinations.

Day 76

"Know then that Rahab lives serenely in
that light, and since her presence joins our order,
she seals that order in the highest rank."

(PARADISO 9.115–117)

A *gain, it's not so much that the presence of souls—or, as Dante has*
been calling these avatars of the Blessed, "splendors"—is odd,
given that each succumbed to their physical passions in their earthly
lives and did not live in perfect purity. The splendor who speaks here,
who identifies himself as Folco, explains to Dante that they have no
memory of their faults, having drunk of the River Lethe before leaving
Purgatory. Instead of the joys of erotic love, these blessed souls merely
relish how the Divine Love works to order everything for the good.
Their proclivity to love intensely has been transformed so that their
privileged understanding of the ways of Providence work in accord
with the highest love of all. This seemingly paradoxical reality is fur-
ther realized in the third heaven because the very first soul to inhabit
this station—released from Limbo in the Harrowing of Hell following
the Crucifixion—and the one who ranks among the highest within it
is the harlot Rahab, who helped the Israelites led by Joshua in subdu-
ing Jericho and then defected to their ranks herself (Joshua 2). And so
a figure who lived a debased existence, practicing "the world's oldest
profession," presumably because of her amorous nature, was able to
refocus her eros on fidelity to and worship of the God who is love.

Day 77

"I was a lamb among the holy flock
that Dominic leads on the path where one
may fatten well if one does not stray off."

(PARADISO 10.94–96)

*In this canto, Dante makes an important transition in his journey:
He enters the celestial spheres that are free of any shadow of the
earth. In the hierarchy of the blessed souls, these begin to form the
choirs that drink most fully of the Divine Nature and Light. Dante
notes that the brightness of these splendors is so intense that they, like
the Sun, in whose sphere they appear, would deprive the unprepared
eye of sight. In this sphere, Dante celebrates the virtue of wisdom. As
Dante and Beatrice arrive, the souls manifested here form a circle
around them, a circle that Dante compares to a crown. The spokes-
man for these souls, who identifies himself in the stanza tweeted
today, is none other than Thomas Aquinas, the well-spring of much
of the theology on which Dante bases his journey and its poetic ac-
count. The first time I read* Paradiso, *this discovery produced both
satisfaction and puzzlement within me. It pleased me to see Dante
introducing Thomas into the poem as a prominent presence; it also
puzzled me that Dante did not place him in a higher sphere, since
Dante reverenced him so. Upon reflection, however, not only does the
choice make sense, but I believe Aquinas himself would be happy to be
so dealt with, given what he taught about the importance of humility,
the habit of knowing and accepting what is true about yourself. Aqui-
nas introduces the luminous presences in the group that circles Dante,
some now obscure. Given who they are, their presence here makes
sense; but Dante does present us with a couple of surprises. For one,
it becomes clear that Solomon makes up one of the lights forming the
circumference of the circle. This seems a "no-brainer" because of his
reputation in scripture as a lover of wisdom, but we also remember
how his amorous nature got him into trouble and ultimately brought*

Israel to ruin. Would he not be better placed in the third heaven of Venus that Dante has just departed? In a later canto, Aquinas will further elucidate his comments about Solomon in Canto 10. Another surprising presence here is the splendor who once was Siger of Brabant, about whom Aquinas speaks admiringly. Because Siger was an avowed Averroist, these two were philosophical opponents, and the Church even censured Siger for teachings that were deemed heretical. But Dante again invokes a different standard than the rulings of the Church hierarchy, as he does with the soul of Manfred in Purgatorio. What matters in the Paradiso depends more on charity than on belonging to certain philosophical camps.

Day 78

O senseless cares of mortals, how deceiving
are syllogistic reasonings that bring
your wings to flight so low, to earthly things!

(PARADISO 11.1–3)

*D*ante opens this canto with an apostrophe. He continues with a
denunciation of the activities that on earth are commonly taken
to be wisdom. These are the practical and pragmatic undertakings
that people commonly think of as leading to earthly prominence and
prosperity. In comparison to what Dante is experiencing at that mo-
ment, however, they appear vain and worthless. Dante's reminder
here of the hierarchy of the goods pursued in wisdom is the perfect
prologue to what follows in the canto. Aquinas intuits that Dante is
confused about two of his earlier statements, one being that which I
have quoted previously when Thomas describes himself as "a lamb
among that holy flock/that Dominic leads on the path where one/
may fatten well if one does not stray off." Thomas addresses Dante's
confusion about this claim by noting how Providence, in a time of the
Church's great need, caused two formidable figures to arise in order
to strengthen her: Dominic and Francis. Out of the fraternal charity
that dwells in the souls of the blessed, Thomas extols the founder of
the Franciscans. His panegyric lauds Francis as being one courageous
enough to take Poverty to be his bride. His renunciation of the mate-
rial riches that so many pursue allowed him to inject new vitality
into the Church and won for him the highest reward: the Stigmata,
by which he shared the marks of Christ's Passion. Aquinas ends the
canto with a lament for how few at that time were willing to maintain
the life of holy poverty that Francis and his earliest followers lived. In
short, he laments that so many in those later times had given their
lives to those same mundane pursuits that Dante denounces at the
outset of the canto. The "lowly cord" (87) that Francis and his follow-
ers wore around their waists reminds us of the rope belt that Dante

wore, which Virgil mysteriously drops into the abyss of the Eighth Circle in Inferno, *whose summoning of Geryon serves as an earlier indicator of how far the order Francis founded may have by that time strayed from its original course.*

Day 79

then from the heart of one of the new lights
there came a voice, and as I turned toward it,
I seemed a needle turning to the polestar;

(PARADISO 12.28-30)

New splendors arrive on the scene to enhance Dante's experience
of the Sun. Another group encircles the group who circled Dante
and Beatrice at first. Dante compares this arrangement to a double
rainbow and relates how the two circles of splendors sing and move
in harmony with one another. A new speaker addresses Dante, one
who says he will complement Thomas' praise of Francis, who founded
the newly arrived speaker's order, by praising Francis' compeer, the
founder of Thomas' order: Dominic. He praises Dominic as one who
sought to purify the Church of heresy, so that the faithful would not be
misled into error by which they might forfeit eternal life in ways that
harmonized with Francis' reforms, carried out through preaching and
teaching. Dominic's mission was one that our own contemporaries
would find distasteful because of the ardor with which he defended
purity of doctrine. Intriguingly, Dante introduces this canto with sev-
eral allusions to classical mythology, culminating with a reference to
the tale of Echo's transformation told by Ovid in his Metamorphoses,
perhaps demonstrating the wide scope that respecting purity of doc-
trine allows in Dante's understanding. After his account of Dominic,
the speaker identifies himself as Bonaventure, Thomas' contemporary
and sometime opponent in the scholastic disputes inspired by the
theological controversies that arose among the faculties of the great
medieval universities. In these cantos their reciprocating eulogies of
the founders of their rival's order dramatize that here they have left
all such disputations behind because now they see clearly and love
infinitely the Divine Wisdom that they experience in their direct vi-
sion of God's essence.

Day 80

"opinion—hasty—often can incline
to the wrong side, and then affection for
one's own opinion binds, confines the mind."

(PARADISO 13.118–120)

*A*lthough its assertion is timeless, the tweeted stanza for Day 80
speaks to our world in a special way. We humans have always
been fond of our opinions, vetted or unvetted; and I suppose that there
has not been an era or a culture in which certain opinions were not
enshrined in ways that led a great number of people to live with minds
that were bound and confined. Recent events only seem to have ampli-
fied this tendency in human nature, creating crises that we might bet-
ter have avoided had we applied some clear thinking to situations that
have aggravated our misfortunes. Worse, it appears that some have in-
tentionally misled large groups of people for their own gain by feeding
them opinions that are patently false as if they were true. At any rate,
in this canto, Thomas Aquinas, who resumes speaking after Bonaven-
ture has ceased, provides a master class in the application of logic and
the art of making distinctions in explaining to Dante his comments on
Solomon in Canto 10, remarks that implied to Dante that Solomon's
wisdom—what Thomas calls his "matchless vision"—was equal, if not
superior to, that of any other human to have lived. That would seem to
make him superior in this regard both to Adam and to Christ. Thomas'
explanation puts his comment into perspective, contextualizing it, as
we would call it now, in order to show that his praise applies to Solo-
mon specifically in the area of kingly wisdom, as opposed to wisdom
in general. Dante concludes the canto with another salutary reminder:
We should refrain from being "too confident/in judging" (130–131),
because, living in a world of flux, we cannot perfectly anticipate the
outcome of events that are in progress. Some things that seem just
within reach of success may fail. Those whose actions seem headed
toward damnation may be saved at the last.

Day 81 (13 September)

Lights moved along that cross from horn to horn
and from the summit to the base, and as
they met and passed, they sparkled, radiant:

(PARADISO 14.109–11)

In the final part of this canto, Dante and Beatrice leave behind the souls whose signature virtue is wisdom and ascend into the fifth sphere of Paradiso, the sphere of Mars. In this zone of heaven, Dante will encounter the splendors of the warriors who fought to defend the faith. These souls, bathed in and glowing with the red hue of the planet, greet Dante arranged in the shape of a cross upon which the Corpus of Christ miraculously flashes forth in a vision that transcends Dante's ability to describe or even to remember it fully. The splendors then break into a melody and hymn that are beyond Dante's capacity to understand, save for a word or two. This hymn picks up the thread of a subject that Dante has been tracing throughout the Commedia, *and on which I've commented before that has to do with language and eloquence. In* Inferno, *Dante several times experiences moments when language loses lucidity and deteriorates into gibberish, as in the encounter with Plutus at the beginning of Canto 7, or with Nimrod, whom Dante portrays as the original corrupter of language by virtue of his role in building the Tower of Babel, in Canto 30. As Dante ascends from sphere-to-sphere in* Paradiso, *he experiences the opposite: Not language that is unintelligible because it is gibberish and subrational, but language that transcends Dante's intelligence because it is suprarational. But just in case we misconstrue and think that the anthem he hears is even more enrapturing than Beatrice, Dante reminds us that it is only because he has yet to turn his eyes toward his Beloved in the sphere of Mars. When he does, it is only to reaffirm that her beauty is even greater than the song he hears and that she grows lovelier with each new sphere they enter, consistent with my earlier note about how, for Dante, Beatrice is the personification of the beauties of*

85

the celestial realm through which he travels. A final note: Before any of this happens, Dante inquires of Thomas what will happen to the splendor of the blessed souls he encounters in Paradise when they are reunited with their bodies at the general resurrection. Thomas affirms that the light in which they are clothed will only intensify at that time with greater glory. This canto thereby also resonates with Canto 6 of Inferno, which ends with Virgil explaining to Dante that the miseries of the damned will increase when their souls and bodies are once again rejoined.

Day 82 (14 September)[3]

"O you, my branch in whom I took delight
even awaiting you, I am your root,"
so he, in his reply to me, began,

(PARADISO 15.88–90)

This verse, indeed the entire Canto, celebrates family pride. More than that, it voices the nostalgia that so many have felt at various times: the longing for "the good old days." This canto is an especially auspicious one for Dante. He has discovered among the splendid presences here the soul of his great-great-grandfather Cacciaguida, who descends from his position on the right transept of the Cross to its foot to celebrate the arrival of and to speak with his descendant. Dante's discovery of Cacciaguida places the root of his family tree firmly in the tree of the Cross and so in the tree of life. His forebear, a member of what can be called Florence's "greatest generation," won a martyr's crown by forfeiting his life in the Crusades. Enthusiasm for the Crusades is not very fashionable today, but to Dante this would have been the equivalent of having a distinguished ancestor who fought with the Allies in the Second World War. Although waning, as the number of those who lived and fought in World War II and are still alive grows progressively smaller, the myth surrounding the defining military conflict of the last century continues to exert great influence. Cacciaguida's account of Florence's "Glory Days," when the residents of that city lived with admirable restraint and moderation reveals Dante's fundamentally declensionist view of history, but it is a view that is tempered with a sense of the glorious destiny toward which the human race moves in a universe ultimately governed by a Providence that holds out the promise of a better world, once the insubstantial and transient goods of earthly life have passed away.

3. Dante died on the night of September 13 or the very early morning of September 14. It is perhaps providential that my tweeting of these cantos in which Dante meets his glorious ancestor coincided with these dates.

87

Day 83

"All things that you possess, possess their death,
just as you do; but in some things that last long,
death can hide from you whose lives are short."

(PARADISO 16.79–81)

*In this stanza, Dante ties civic pride with familial pride. Continuing
the theme of the golden days of Florence from the previous canto,
Cacciaguida responds to Dante's expression of family pride and his
request for a roll call of the prominent names that made up Flor-
ence's citizens in Cacciaguida's day. Dante knows that it is a pride
that carries with it a touch of vanity, but Beatrice indulges Dante as
he continues to speak to Cacciaguida, addressing him in Italian with
the honorific "You." With the remark made in the tweeted stanza for
this day, Dante's ancestor informs him that a number of the names he
is about to pronounce may have disappeared from memory since the
time when Cacciaguida lived until Dante's day. His remark speaks to
the transient nature of fame and reminds us that Dante here is receiv-
ing a favor that is an accommodation to someone who still dwells in
the earthly sphere. What comes through clearly here is that Dante
still harbors a love for his native city and mourns the corrupt state of
that city in his own day by having his forefather reminisce about the
nobility of Florence in its heyday.*

Day 84

"You shall—beside him—see one who, at birth,
had so received the seal of this strong star
that what he does will be remarkable."

(PARADISO 17.76–78)

*The verse for this day constitutes part of the canto that begins with
an allusion to the story of Phaeton found in Ovid's* Metamorphoses,
*in which Dante completes the contrast between early Florence and
latter-day Florence. It comes in the context of Dante's asking Cac-
ciaguida, with Beatrice's urging and full approval, about the various
obscure prophecies that have been made for Dante along the way, by
figures that he meets both in the Inferno and Purgatorio, of some great
future misfortune that he will suffer. He requests that his ancestor
give these oracles their decisive interpretation openly, sparing Dante
nothing of the truth. Dante has steeled himself to hear this prophecy
pronounced by one who can read all of the contingencies of earthly life
in the Divine Essence, shown there not as if fated or destined, but as
foreknown. The luminosity who is Dante's great-great grandfather tells
it to Dante straight: Enemies in Florence intriguing with the Holy See
will strike out against Dante, resulting in his banishment from Flor-
ence. Cacciaguida, speaking some of the most iconic lines in the poem,
tells Dante, "You are to know the bitter taste/of others' bread, how
salt it is, and know/how hard a path it is for one who goes/descending
and ascending others' stairs" (57–60). But there will be consolations:
Dante will receive comfort in his exile from great ones of Italy who are
sympathetic to his plight. In one of the houses that will shelter him, he
will meet a prodigy, a youth who, when he comes of age, will set things
right in the troubled land. This part of Cacciaguida's prophecy that
incorporates today's tweet clearly points to Can Grande della Scala,
the Lombard noble who would become such a valued patron to Dante
that Dante would dedicate the present canticle of* Paradise *to him. The*

words Cacciaguida speaks about this nobleman resonate with Virgil's prophesied "Greyhound" who is to drive the she-wolf that kept Dante from climbing the Blissful Mountain in Canto 1 of Inferno from Italy. In Dante's reply to his forbear, he promises that he will have the best revenge against corrupt Florence: He will achieve such fame as a poet by setting down truly and with eloquence the great poem that will result from his journey, no matter who may suffer from the truth of his account. Based on the acclaim he still enjoys, it seems that Dante did, indeed, get the last laugh.

Day 85

With each light settled quietly in place,
I saw that the array of fire had shaped
the image of an eagle's head and neck.

(PARADISO 18.106–108)

*T*oday's *stanza marks the climactic moment of this transitional
canto, in which Dante travels into the next of the celestial spheres.
The first half of the canto finds Dante still in the sphere of Mars. His
final experience there is Cacciaguida's introduction to Dante of some
of the other remarkable splendors who occupy the figure of the Cross
in this sphere, all warriors of renown from either scripture or history.
Following the heaven of Mars with that of Jupiter, suffused with a
silvery light as opposed to the red glow of Mars, is a logical move.
The justice of the good ruler succeeds the martial valor of the war-
rior. With the transition comes a more dynamic celestial light show
than even the impressive and inspiring Cross bearing Christ's corpus
of the fifth sphere provided. Keeping in mind what Dante learns in
the sphere of the Moon about the souls of the blessed making them-
selves known to Dante in the celestial spheres as what we would call
avatars, would it be unreasonable to compare Dante's portrayal of the
physical heavens to an immense virtual reality stage, anticipating the
developments of that digital technology by several hundred years? The
VR effects here continue as the luminous presences of the just souls
shape themselves into letters that spell out the first verse of the Old
Testament Book of Wisdom. Letter-by-letter they spell out the words
in Latin, words that enjoin the rulers of the earth to love justice. After
adding a flourish to the "O" that makes part of that statement, with
a facility comparable to a precision-drill marching band showcased
in a great celestial halftime show, they then form themselves into the
symbol of the empire that Dante so reveres: the Imperial Eagle that
will speak to Dante with a corporate voice in the next canto.*

Day 86

Wheeling, the Eagle sang, then said: "Even
as are my songs to you—past understanding—
such is Eternal Judgment to you mortals."

(PARADISO 19.97–99)

*T*he subject of this day's stanza takes up the knotty question of
Divine Justice. Dante remains troubled by a concern that has
a direct bearing on his revered Virgil's fate: Why would a virtuous
person who, through no fault of her own, remained unbaptized be
condemned when her life ends? It's a question that a number of my
own students have been moved to ask. It's a question that I myself
have asked, at least as it applies to the scheme of Dante's story. The
Eagle, speaking in a voice in which many speak as one, divines that
this question is on Dante's mind. Its answer, as may be expected, is
that God and God's will and justice are ultimately unfathomable to
humans given that the Divine Nature infinitely transcends human
intellect. However, the answer takes an unexpected turn as the Eagle
further explains. The mere fact of redemption may not be the only
angle from which to approach this question. Echoing Matthew 7:21,
the Eagle affirms that at the Judgment, many of the unbaptized will
fare far better than those "who now cry 'Christ! Christ!'" (121). The
next stanza reads just ambiguously enough to suggest the possibility
that those who did not know Christ, but lived virtuously, will be fa-
vored in a way that will put believers who have turned to wickedness
to shame when all are separated into two "collegi" (110)—"the one
forever rich, the other poor" (111). Just what that way will be cannot
be known yet, but this is the Eagle of Justice speaking, so it must be a
promising resolution to the perplexing problem that troubles Dante.
The next canto will build on that suggestion and take it two steps
further than Dante—or we ourselves—expected.

Day 87

"More than a thousand years before baptizing,
to baptize him there were the same three women
you saw along the chariot's right-hand side."

(PARADISO 20.127–129)

*D*ante's humanism emerges in these stanzas in the ultimate rec-
onciliation of classical with Christian culture to be found in
the story. Having had to accept in the previous canto that the divine
decree about the fate of the unbaptized is just because it originates in
God's will, which is coextensive with His love, and an ambiguous as-
surance that the unbaptized may indeed be rewarded for their merit
in a way that renders them superior to believers who find themselves
condemned for their evil choices and actions, Dante now receives news
that truly astounds him. The Eagle avatar of the Just in the heaven of
Jupiter explains to Dante that the "flames" of the most just among
their souls of light make up the eye of the Eagle. The number of "living
lights" who reside in the eye is six. The Eagle identifies each. Four of
the six, anyone would expect to be there; however, the first and the
fifth who make up the Eagle's brow seem unlikely, if not impossible,
additions to the group. The first is the Roman emperor Trajan, who
supposedly was recalled from the dead by the prayers of Pope Gregory
the Great. Upon returning to the earthly life from the Inferno, he be-
comes a Christian, so that when he leaves this life permanently, he
ascends to his appropriate station in Paradise. The sixth figure is even
more strange; for it is the soul of Ripheus, a Trojan prince, whom Vir-
gil had described as having an intense love of justice. Unlike Trajan,
who at least lived after the birth of Christ, Ripheus lived well before
the Savior's coming and the institution of Baptism. According to the
Eagle here, however, Ripheus' burning love of righteousness led to a
revelation granted to him by Grace that in turn led to a figurative
baptism by "the same three women/[Dante] saw along the chariot's
right-hand side" (121–2), who personify the theological virtues of

faith, hope, and charity. The case of Ripheus puts to rest in a decisive way the doubt troubling Dante in the previous canto concerning the justice of the need of Baptism for salvation, by suggesting that, though a rare instance, God's predestination has defeated the ordinary limitations of time and space so that Ripheus' merit can be duly rewarded with an apotheosis among the souls of the just.

Day 88

"Not much of mortal life was left to me
when I was sought for, dragged to take that hat
which always passes down from bad to worse."

(PARADISO 21.124–126)

*T*he twenty-first canto takes as its central concern the limitation of
human nature and intelligence. In earlier cantos, notably in the
sphere of the sun, Dante reports experiences that transcend his ability
to understand, mostly the songs and utterances of the splendors who
are represented in the higher spheres. Dante has so matched his style—
a style that ranges from the scatalogical to the eschatalogical—to the
experiences he reports that a reader finds herself or himself struggling
more and more with the difficulty of the poem in these final cantos of
Paradiso. As this canto begins, Dante continues the ascent into the
seventh sphere, that of Saturn, expanding the limits of his mortal na-
ture even further. When Dante asks Beatrice why she does not smile
in this sphere, she answers, with yet another allusion to Ovid, that
Dante would be incinerated like Semele if he were to see her smile at
that point. In contrast to the spheres Dante has experienced thus far,
the splendors are silent here. When Dante asks the living light who
was Peter Damian why, he responds that they remain silent for the
same reason that Beatrice has withheld her smile. Peter is one of the
living lights who have been ascending and descending a ladder that
extends into this sphere from above. He has come to welcome Dante
but informs Dante not to inquire any further into the reason for his
being there, for no created being is able to penetrate the depths of the
Divine Wisdom that orders everything. These various references to
things that transcend human nature and intelligence remind us that
Dante now is visiting the sphere where the souls of contemplatives
manifest themselves to him. The ladder is Jacob's Ladder that leads
to an even higher station, farther removed from earth and from the
things of the earth. Peter's words in the stanza featured conclude the

canto with a note that disparages the papal throne, not as the seat of Christ's vicar, but as a seat of human honors and status, unworthy of those whose focus should be elsewhere.

Day 89

The little threshing floor
that so incites our savagery was all—
from hills to river mouths—revealed to me
while I wheeled with eternal Gemini.

(PARADISO 22.150–153)

In today's stanza, Dante's theme of transcendence becomes full-on contemptus mundi. Swept up the ladder that ultimately ends in the Empyrean, after Dante meets and converses with the luminous presence of Benedict of Nursia who decries the corruption of his rule and the order that he founded, Dante enters the sphere of fixed stars under the sign of his birth: Gemini. From that vantage, Beatrice instructs Dante to look down in order to see in a panoramic view to what heights she has brought him. Dante sees how insignificant the earth appears, as he enjoys the majesties of the heavens he has visited so far. His entry into the Fixed Stars under Gemini signifies that he has been born anew, that he has finally realized the "Vita Nuova" the initiation to which he had experienced on a street of his native city where he beheld the young Beatrice. Having attained this station, Dante firmly grasps how precious this new life is and how worthy of scorn are the things that we vainly treasure here on earth that can distract us from it. The hierarchy of his loves has been almost completely reordered since that moment when he awoke to find himself lost in a dark forest.

Day 90

this is no crossing for a little bark—
the sea that my audacious prow now cleaves—
nor for a helmsman who would spare himself.

(PARADISO 23.67–69)

*B*eatrice has been thus far the finite presence that reflects the
celestial glories Dante has been experiencing as he traverses
Paradise, a reflection of the sacramental nature and technique of
Dante's poetry. Having prepared Dante by directing his eyes to the
transforming visions of the highest spheres, Beatrice now bestows on
him the smile that she had denied him for his own safety in the previ-
ous canto. He survives the imparting of this favor; but, as will happen
more frequently now as his journey advances, the vision of its beauty
outstrips the power of his mortal tongue to render it in words. But just
as he drinks in the wonder of the high privilege Beatrice has afforded
him, she admonishes him not to let her face distract him from the
other glories that surround him in this sphere. In this way, Beatrice
is preparing Dante for that moment when she will have to step aside
and give way to the substance of the glory of which she herself is a
sign. When Dante obeys her, he sees a rare vision of the souls of the
blessed portrayed as a garden, with the Mother of God the finest rose
therein. About her circles the angelic messenger of the Annunciation
who, in honoring her thus, makes a crown. While still beholding this
sight, Dante and the rest of the company ascend once again to the
next sphere, bringing Dante that much closer to the fulfillment and
completion of his journey.

Day 91

This done, the high and holy court resounded
throughout its spheres with "Te Deum laudamus,"
sung with the melody they use on high.

(PARADISO 24.112–114)

*T*he cause for celebration depicted in the stanza for today's tweet
caps Dante's examination in the theological virtue of Faith. His
examiner is none other than Peter the Apostle, the keeper of the keys
of the Kingdom. Beatrice has asked the assembled company who sur-
round herself and Dante among the Fixed Stars to "direct your mind
to his immense desire,/quench him somewhat" (7–8). In yet another
display of the magnificent symmetry with which Dante organizes his
tale, the holy avatars at this point take on the form of flaming spheres
spinning around fixed poles, an image that correlates to the spherical
dance of the cosmos that emanates from the Divine Love. Peter comes
forth and welcomes Beatrice by spinning around her, paralleling Ga-
briel's display of homage to Mary in the last canto. Then Peter puts
Dante to the test, a test that Dante compares to a student undergoing
the examination for a bachelor's degree, conducted in the Scholastic
style, the setting from which Dante's admiration of Aristotle derived.
Dante handily passes the examination, basing his answer to Peter's
inquiry on the text of Hebrews 11:1; but like any good and thorough
examiner, Peter requires Dante to make distinctions and to qualify
and define the key terms of his response. And so, in the midst of one
of the moments of highest mysticism in the story, Dante wonderfully
folds into the mystical experience the logical methods inspired by "the
master of those who know." In a move that may surprise those who
misunderstand the Middle Ages, he also acknowledges the primacy
of the scriptures as a source of the faith he professes. It is one of the
reasons why readers of all denominations should be able to appreciate
Dante's poem. In fact, a wide diversity of readers have held, and do
hold, Dante's poetry in high esteem.

Day 92

"'May those'—he says within his theody—
'who know Your name, put hope in You'; and if
one has my faith, can he not know God's name?"

(PARADISO 25.73–75)

*T*he next examiner to test Dante approaches in much the same
manner that Peter had. The second flaming sphere belongs to
James, who comes to inquire into the soundness of Dante's knowledge
and possession of hope. Upon James' questioning of Dante, Beatrice
speaks up for the pupil and notes that Dante's very presence in this
place and the inspiration for his journey both give evidence of Dante's
possession of hope. But Dante has more to answer for than the simple
fact of his hope. He must also explain the origin and nourishment
of this hope, as well as what it is that hope promised. The opening of
Dante's response is captured in the verse for today. Dante answers that
it sparked first from Psalm 9 quoted here, as well as from the Epistle
authored by James himself in the New Testament. After satisfying this
auditor, a third and final examiner arrives in the same way as the
other two. The third, and last, of these examiners who try Dante's
worthiness to continue his journey into the Empyrean will be none
other than John, the brother of James, who along with Peter made
up the three disciples to whom Jesus entrusted both some of the key
moments of his ministry and the care of his Church in the Gospels. His
examination of Dante continues in the next canto.

Day 93

"The leaves enleaving all the garden of
the Everlasting Gardener, I love
according to the good He gave to them."

(PARADISO 26.64–66)

*T*he stanza tweeted for today stands as part of Dante's response to
John's examination of Dante on the topic of love. As this canto
begins, Dante remains blind, having consumed his eyesight trying
to penetrate the light in which the Evangelist is shrouded to see the
lineaments of his physical features. Undeterred by Dante's temporary
vision loss, John tests Dante on his understanding of love. This will be
the culminating examination on which the conclusion of his journey
depends. The stakes seem high; but, as mentioned above, the purpose
of his journey has been to reorder the hierarchy of his loves. After
establishing that only the good is worthy to be loved, and that the
only highest good is worthy of the highest form of love, Dante ac-
knowledges that created things also deserve love in the same measure
that the created goodness they carry within them can in turn draw
us to the love of their Creator. This acknowledgement constitutes yet
another affirmation of Dante's sacramental view of the world. The
examination ends successfully, and Beatrice restores and strength-
ens Dante's eyesight with the power of her gaze. The earlier loss of
his sight, then, was a preparation for the even greater marvels that
Dante is about to witness. At first Dante comments on the enhanced
strength of vision he enjoys when Beatrice clears his eyes. In addition,
he perceives a new presence, a fourth, who has joined the venerable
company formed by the splendors of Peter, James, and John: our first
father, Adam, who answers some questions from Dante. Dante doesn't
state these wishes explicitly, but Adam intuits Dante's questions even
before he has a chance to speak them. Adam briefs Dante on his per-
sonal history, but also remarks on the language that he spoke. Adam's
comments on language stand in direct contrast to Dante's assertions

in his uncompleted treatise, De Vulgari Eloquentia, *in which Dante conjectures that the original language of Eden didn't change until the episode of the Tower of Babel, when all tongues were confused as a consequence of human presumption. Here, Adam relates that the primal language had changed prior to Babel. The first father also reports, in a way that deflates human pretensions and presumptuousness, that it wasn't long past the sixth hour of his existence in the Earthly Paradise, that he transgressed and so lost Eden for himself and for all of his descendents.*

Day 94

"This heaven has no other where than this:
the mind of God, in which are kindled both
the love that turns it and the force it rains."

(PARADISO 27.109–111)

*B*eatrice *and Dante have finally entered the ninth sphere of the Paradiso: the Primum Mobile. This is where the created universe both begins and ends, hence, Beatrice's description of its location within "the mind of God." Prior to Dante's becoming aware that he has entered this sphere, he listens to Peter's denunciation of the corrupt papacy that at that time ruled the Church, one motivated by increasing its own wealth and power, as opposed to caring for the souls of its flock and embracing the holy poverty in which the apostles lived. Both Peter and Beatrice speak of a reckoning, which will eventually set things right again. There is a strong suggestion that that reckoning will come with a restoration of the Empire, which will root vice both from the spiritual and secular realms. At any rate, Peter's condemnation implies that said reckoning cannot come soon enough for his taste. The Primum Mobile serves as the mediator between the Creator and the rest of his created world. It is where both time and the power of the other spheres raining down on creation to ensure differentiation among the contingent beings that fill the universe originate. It turns at a far greater speed than all the other spheres, receiving its motive force from God Himself. This will be Dante's final stop before he transcends nature completely and enters the Empyrean where God, the angels, and the blessed actually reside as essences and not as avatars or spectacles created as accommodations for Dante's senses and imagination.*

Day 95

My lady, who saw my perplexity—
I was in such suspense—said: "On that Point
depend the heavens and the whole of nature."

(PARADISO 28.40–42)

In this canto Dante calls Beatrice "the lady who imparadises/my mind"
(1–2). At this point, each new revelation is preceded by Dante gazing
on Beatrice, as if in preparation for the next wonder that he will perceive.
Still in the Primum Mobile, once Dante turns his eyes from Beatrice's
face to what surrounds him, he perceives a point of light, encircled by
nine rings of fire. As Beatrice explains here, the point (or Point) is the
Godhead; the rings that wheel around the Point are the nine orders of
angels. Dante's perplexity increases, however, when Beatrice explains to
him that the highest orders circle the central Point more closely, and at
a faster rate of speed, than the lower orders, which seems just the op-
posite of the way in which Dante has experienced the order of the created
universe. Dante begins the canto with a simile involving the perception
of a mirrored flame, and Beatrice's explanation seems to build upon the
pattern of mirror reversal first broached in the simile. Her explanation
depends on the introduction of matter into the construction of the cre-
ated universe, maintaining that more power requires a greater amount
of matter to embody it. This same condition would not hold for the
heaven that transcends matter, where proximity to the Alpha point of
the universe reflects a greater likeness to God and greater love of God.
The canto ends with a short digression on the orders of the angels and the
controversy in the early Church about their arrangement involving alter-
nate explanations by Pseudo-Dionysius and Gregory the Great. Beatrice
confirms that Pseudo-Dionysius was correct and Gregory was not, add-
ing the charming detail that, when Gregory was able to view his error
upon his arrival in Paradise, he smiled at his mistake. This account sug-
gests a certain levity among the souls of the elect that recalls Chesterton's
aphorism, "The angels can fly because they can take themselves lightly."

Day 96

"By now you see the height, you see the breadth,
of the Eternal Goodness: It has made
so many mirrors, which divide Its light,
but, as before, Its own Self still is One."

(PARADISO 29.142–145)

*T*he tweeted verse for today sums up Beatrice's discourse on the choirs of the angels, with which she instructs Dante to correct several errors made by theologians and preachers about the creation of the angels, the creation of the cosmos, the rebellion of Lucifer, and the way in which the Divine Love is distributed among the angels who circle the Omega Point in constant contemplation, claiming that each angel receives that love in a way unique from all the rest, despite being grouped into nine orders. Whereas each of the angels and all things in creation reflect the Divine Love in varying degrees, the Point that constitutes the beginning and end of time and space, although existing outside of time and space, possesses uniquely the essence of that love. As Dante inhabits the threshold that is the final divide between time and eternity and must be prepared for the experience of what is always and everywhere true, Beatrice denounces those who distort those truths, whether out of ignorance or malevolence. He must be worthy of the high privilege he is about to receive. Beatrice must make clear his eyes of any potential error that could cloud his vision or understanding of what has yet been revealed to him.

Day 97

There, near and far do not subtract or add;
for where God governs with no mediator,
no thing depends upon the laws of nature.

(PARADISO 30.121–123)

In the verse tweeted on this day, it is as if Dante, taking us along with him, has entered a mystical region that resembles an icon or the dazzling mosaics found in the apse of a Gothic or Romanesque cathedral. In such works, the absence of perspective, of the illusion of proximity and distance, suggests to the beholder the effect of having entered eternity, beyond time and dimension. Dante relates a similar experience upon entering the Empyrean. According to Beatrice, whose beauty now exceeds the ability of Dante's words to praise her, they now are in "the heaven of pure light" (39), but it is not a physical light. Rather it is "Light of the intellect" (40). At this point, Dante has reached a moment that finds its parallel in Canto 30 of Purgatorio: as with Virgil earlier, Beatrice's work is almost finished. She directs Dante to cleanse his eyes one final time in a stream of pure "light that takes a river's form" (61). After he does so, he begins to perceive things in a different way and sees what looks to be an enormous rose. In place of petals, there are tiers occupied by the souls of the blessed, illuminated by a sun from which the light of God itself shines. The position that each of the blessed inhabits indicates the degree of her or his holiness and to what extent each receives and reflects the light of God, although each is bathed in its life-giving rays. As earthly flowers thrive and grow in the light of our sun, so the light of that heavenly Sun invests each with eternal light and allows each to bask in everlasting glory.

Day 98

Where I expected her, another answered:
I thought I should see Beatrice, and saw
an elder dressed like those who are in glory.

(PARADISO 31.58–60)

*O*nce Dante has entered the Empyrean, Beatrice who has embod-
ied for Dante the glory of the physical heavens and of the cre-
ated world, having been reunited with Dante in the Earthly Paradise,
finally leaves Dante's side and returns to her place in the Mystical
Rose just as Virgil leaves Dante and returns to Limbo once Beatrice
appears on the summit of Purgatory. Unlike Virgil, however, Beatrice
does not disappear. Her departure may surprise Dante, as he sees
in her place a venerable old man, who turns out to be Bernard of
Clairvaux; however, she has merely returned to her ordained place
in the White Rose, which Dante has just described in some detail.
Paradoxically, her distance from Dante is both very far and very near.
Although she is no longer next to him, Dante can see her as clearly as
if she were. She turns her eyes to Dante a final time before turning her
face decisively toward the Divine Light that she reflects and in which
she and the other blessed souls find, not only their glory, but the very
source of their being. Bernard, whom Dante knows to be an ardent
devotee of the Mother of God, bids Dante to turn his eyes upon Mary.
On doing so, he gazes in wonder at the angels sporting around the
place where she sits in the Rose, described by Dante with another al-
lusion to Ovid, which shines more brightly than any of its other petals.

Day 99

And the angelic love who had descended
earlier, now spread his wings before her,
singing "Ave Maria, gratia plena."

(PARADISO 32.94–96)

*T*hroughout the Commedia *one facet of Dante's quest has been the
redemption of his amorous disposition as a love poet. This thread
of the poem can be detected in such moments as Dante's encounter
with Francesca and Paolo in Canto V of* Inferno *in which Francesca
maintains that love is irresistible, a meeting that results in his fainting
after their visit to the dream of the Siren in* Purgatorio *to the necessity
of being engulfed among the lyric poets in the purifying flame on the
terrace of Lust as one of the final steps of his own purgation to Bea-
trice's accusations of Dante's infidelity of which he fully repents in the
Earthly Paradise. Upon Dante's entry into the Empyrean, as we noted,
Beatrice herself has retreated from her place at Dante's side to her
place in the Mystical Rose of the Blessed. As his new guide Bernard
of Clairvaux makes clear while explaining to Dante the composition
of said Rose, we learn that, although Beatrice is afforded a high place
within, hers is not the highest position, being of the third degree.
Dante's devotion to Beatrice, then, has led to this moment of transcen-
dence, when Beatrice herself steps aside from her role as mediatrix
and directs his devotion to its true end. Replacing her in the economy
of Dante the lover's salvation as the ultimate mediatrix of grace, and
the proper focus of his affection, is Mary herself, as Dante sees now
while being instructed by Mary's most devoted adherent, Bernard.
The canto ends with Bernard on the verge of making his propitiatory
prayer to the Virgin Mary for her intercession in strengthening Dante
for his vision of the Highest Love.*

Day 100 (October 2)

Here force failed my high fantasy; but my
desire and will were moved already—like
a wheel revolving uniformly—by
the Love that moves the sun and the other stars.

(PARADISO 33.142–145)

Conventional, perhaps, but there is no way that my final tweet would not be a quotation of the four most famous final lines of almost any known work of literature. Of course, as with almost every other canto, there is so much that could epitomize the contents of the entire piece. A very close second in my mind would be the opening lines of the canto, Bernard's prayer for the Blessed Virgin's intercession to allow Dante's eyes to be strengthened enough to enjoy the Beatific Vision, the goal of his great journey. This prayer, beginning with the memorable paradox, "'Virgin Mother, daughter of your Son," and in which all heaven joins silently, including and especially Beatrice, serves as the ultimate invocation of the epic Dante has constructed. And even though along the way, Dante concludes, concurring with Aquinas, that knowledge precedes love, the culmination of his adventure is the experience of being completely enfolded by the cosmic Love that is the source and end of all creation.

Postscript

First, thank you to everyone who persevered with me through the entire journey. Thanks also to anyone who followed and responded in any small way on Twitter while my undertaking was in progress.

Dante completes the pilgrimage that begins in the Dark Forest and leads him through the hellscape of Inferno, through the alpine rigors of Purgatory, on to the realms of celestial radiance; however, once achieving his exalted destination, he doesn't remain there. After experiencing the ineffable bliss of the Beatific Vision, he is returned to the troubled "threshing floor" from which he started in order to make a record of his journey so that others can join him. Using his mastery of eloquence and poetic technique, especially through what some would refer to as the "tropological level" of the poem's polysemous interpretation, Dante gives us an allegorical portrait and an anatomy of the human soul when it is in bondage to sin, as it struggles to escape the grip of evil, and as it finally emerges free and clear from darkness enabled to embrace the light of the greatest good. At journey's end, Dante sends us back to earth, as well. His task as a poet completed, he restores us to our lives of toil, trouble, struggle, and sometimes triumph with the glories of his poem to nourish us and to "imparadise" our minds.

Works Consulted

Alighieri, Dante. *The Divine Comedy.* Translated by Allen Mandelbaum. New York, NY: Everyman Library, 1995.

Columbia University Libraries. "Digital Dante." *http://digitaldante.columbia. edu.*

De Wulf, Maurice. "Siger of Brabant." *The Catholic Encyclopedia.* Vol. 13. New York:

Robert Appleton Company, 1912. 16 Nov. 2021 <http://www.newadvent.org/ cathen/13784a.htm>.

The Institute for Advanced Technologies in the Humanities. University of Virginia. "The World of Dante." *http://www.worldofdante.org/index.html*